Apologies from
a Repentant Christian

Donna L. Young

TABLE OF CONTENTS

I dedicate this book to God,
His only Son: my Savior Jesus Christ
and the Holy Spirit who now lives within me.

FOREWORD

I f you are like me, you sometimes read the forward or first chapter of a book before deciding whether to continue reading. If you do this too, I am sure you will find it convenient that I have summarized my testimony right up front. If you decide to continue reading, I hope that God touches your life through the following chapters. Thank you for reading about my transformation. Thank you for reading my story.

My life seemed normal until a week prior to October 20, 2008. For just under a week, I prayed for a purpose in life. One night, I found myself watching a special on television. The program featured doctors from the United States helping sufferers in Haiti. I began to pray, "Please God, use my life to bring others to You." Since I had participated in mission trips before, I really felt God would send me on another short-term mission. Perhaps I would go unaccompanied, seeing that my husband of five years and I had grown apart. His unbelief, as well as, his addiction to prescription medication had severed my desire to bring *him* to Christ any longer.

Four days after praying for God to use me, my husband overdosed on prescription medication and physically hurt me. Although our marriage had been failing for years, prior to this date, my husband had never raised a hand to me. When I called the Sheriff's department to report the incident, my husband put on his Navy uniform, greeted the deputies and lied about what happened. The young Sheriff's deputies believed my husband's lies. Consequently, I was charged with a felony and restrained from my home, belongings and more importantly, my three-year-old son. My life was changed from that moment on. Out of sheer desperation, I turned to Jesus for help and finally acknowledged that He is with me through my trials. I began to trust Him.

While hunched over in a jail holding cell, I surrendered my life to Christ and He immediately responded. Jesus spoke to me through another inmate who offered me instant comfort and assurance. Just after the young woman entered the holding cell, she looked right at me and said in a slang drawl, "Girl, why you cryin,' God's with you," and then started to sing old church hymns. I stopped crying and asked her for her name. She simply replied, "It's t."

God was also in the Jail Supervisor who put her hand on my shoulder and very softly said, "You are going to get through this." The same officer "accidentally" allowed me to wear my cross necklace while I was in the holding cell. The tower watchman treated me as a guest and yelled for me to call my mother, whom he had already spoken to. Soon bail was paid. The Supervisor released me from the holding cell and allowed me to wait in the lobby for my parents to arrive.

I began to notice how God had orchestrated the event. The criminal attorney I hired was well known by the judge and prosecuting attorney. He cut me a large break in his normal fees and had the charges dropped as quickly as possible. The doctor who treated my injuries wrote his report to corroborate with my story. Childhood friends from my home town went out of their way to show God's mercy. And a grocery store clerk said something personal and encouraging that only God would have known to say.

Through the hope and help from Jesus during this incident, my heart began to transform. Many years of arrogance and self-righteousness erased quickly. I no longer wanted to be the center of attention. I learned to surrender to God's will, and boy was I humbled.

Because of the violence with my husband, I did move out of our home and into a small apartment with our youngest son. I invited my stepson to move with us but he chose to remain with his father. Initially, my husband refused to get help for his addiction or admit what he had done. Out of frustration, I met with a divorce attorney. I prayed before the meeting and while listening to the attorney talk about the details of a divorce, I had an overwhelming sense not to proceed. Consequently, I did not divorce my husband. Instead, I enrolled in school. As God would have it, the program I entered was Theological

Seminary. I began to learn Scripture for the first time. Then, God became my center of attention.

I started to pray for my husband again. Amazingly, on his own, he sought the help of a therapist. And, after five years of never wanting anything to do with God; he began to attend church.

My husband has since accepted Jesus into his life and even encouraged my recent baptism and graduation from the Seminarian program. He professes his faith daily to others. He has even tattooed his arm with a picture of a bible inside praying hands as part of his testimony to the changes in him.

Prior to this incident, I would say that I trusted God, but usually found myself still trying to control every situation. I no longer struggle with control and have since learned what it means to trust in God and truly surrender. I also learned that when we pray for God to use us, He may answer in a way never expected.

I have walked hand in hand with Jesus for the past two years. He has spoken to me through scripture and spiritual songs. He has even used people to speak His Word to reach my heart. God has used this trial in my life to lead several of my neighbors, friends, family and the homeless to Him. He has even reunited me with my biological father, who, until recently, I had not spoken to in over 23 years.

October 20, 2008 was a night I will never forget! What I initially thought was the worst night of my life turned out to be the night I discovered profound love. It was the night that began the greatest love story I've ever known; the one between Jesus and me.

God can work miracles when we surrender our life to Him. My life is a testimony of His love. He has compelled me to apologize to those I offended with my past behavior, attitude and words. I am writing this book as a sincere apology from the repentant heart of a transformed Christian.

PRAYER

Abba Father, you have chosen me to be an instrument in reaching others with Your Word and this story. May this book reflect your heart and reach each person the moment they need *YOU* the most. Father, please give me wisdom to speak Your Word correctly. Help me to lead people closer to you. Please let my story provide help and hope for the brokenhearted, humbleness for the proud and direction for the confused.

Father, I pray that this book honors You and is part of your will. Please let its purpose be to bless others. Thank you for your perfect Son, in whose name I pray.

Amen.

CHAPTER ONE

I PRAYED WITH A DESIRE TO DO GOD'S WILL

I used to think, "If anyone truly saw the depths of my heart, they'd abandon me." I simply couldn't risk feeling the same rejection I felt as a child. For much of my life, I frightened others away from me with defensiveness and a self-righteous attitude. I felt a hopeless separation from God. Yet, at the same time, I called myself a Christian. I wore a cross around my neck and attended church almost every Sunday. In the darkest hour of my life, on October 20, 2008, God created a new heart in me. I disabled my defenses and ran to God for protection. God opened my eyes and allowed me to see my own reflection through the eyes of the world. In a very precious moment, He allowed me to see His holiness and then worked through others to show me His intentions for a virtuous, loving and compassionate Christian woman.

As I began this new journey in my life, God kept the memory of my past behavior on the surface of my heart. My new journey included a desire to encourage and build up His people. I prayed, "Please God, help me reach out to others."

Then I turned to scripture for answers. I took hold of the spine of my bible and let the pages fall open. As the pages settled, my eyes were drawn to 'chapter 30' in the book of Isaiah. I started to read, and was I surprised! Through all my years of pain and suffering, God had been patiently waiting for me to come to Him for help. I smiled when I read verses regarding God's ability to answer prayer (30:18-19), His guidance (30:20-21), His cleansing (30:22), fruitfulness (30:23-26), victory (30:27-33) and song (30:29).

God keeps His promises! Through repentance, God has forgiven me. He has blessed me by answering my prayers. He has provided guidance and cleansed my heart. Today, I can attest to the words found in Isaiah chapter 30. I used to think, "If anyone truly saw the depths of my heart, they'd abandon me." Now, I can't wait to share my transformed heart with others.

CHAPTER TWO

I BECAME CONSCIOUS OF HOW I LED OTHERS AWAY FROM CHRIST

I promised myself to pray and turn to scripture before writing each of the chapters of this book. Through a humble heart, I asked God "Will You please help me write words that convey a message of hope?" Then when I opened my bible, I read Chapter 11, of Proverbs, which says:

¹ Dishonest scales *are* an abomination to the LORD, But a just weight *is* His delight.
² When pride comes, then comes shame; But with the humble *is* wisdom.
³ The integrity of the upright will guide them, But the perversity of the unfaithful will destroy them.

[4] Riches do not profit in the day of wrath,
But righteousness delivers from death.
[5] The righteousness of the blameless will direct his way aright,
But the wicked will fall by his own wickedness.
[6] The righteousness of the upright will deliver them,
But the unfaithful will be caught by *their* lust.
[7] When a wicked man dies, *his* expectation will perish,
And the hope of the unjust perishes.
[8] The righteous is delivered from trouble,
And it comes to the wicked instead.
[9] The hypocrite with *his* mouth destroys his neighbor,
But through knowledge the righteous will be delivered.
[10] When it goes well with the righteous, the city rejoices;
And when the wicked perish, *there is* jubilation.
[11] By the blessing of the upright the city is exalted,
But it is overthrown by the mouth of the wicked.
[12] He who is devoid of wisdom despises his neighbor,
But a man of understanding holds his peace.
[13] A talebearer reveals secrets,
But he who is of a faithful spirit conceals a matter.
[14] Where *there is* no counsel, the people fall;
But in the multitude of counselors *there is* safety.
[15] He who is surety for a stranger will suffer,
But one who hates being surety is secure.
[16] A gracious woman retains honor,
But ruthless *men* retain riches.
[17] The merciful man does good for his own soul,
But *he who is* cruel troubles his own flesh.

[18] The wicked *man* does deceptive work,
But he who sows righteousness *will have* a sure reward.
[19] As righteousness *leads* to life,
So he who pursues evil *pursues it* to his own death.
[20] Those who are of a perverse heart *are* an abomination to the LORD,
But *the* blameless in their ways *are* His delight.
[21] *Though they join* forces, the wicked will not go unpunished;
But the posterity of the righteous will be delivered.
[22] *As* a ring of gold in a swine's snout,
So is a lovely woman who lacks discretion.
[23] The desire of the righteous *is* only good,
But the expectation of the wicked *is* wrath.
[24] There is *one* who scatters, yet increases more;
And there is *one* who withholds more than is right,
But it *leads* to poverty.
[25] The generous soul will be made rich,
And he who waters will also be watered himself.
[26] The people will curse him who withholds grain,
But blessing *will be* on the head of him who sells *it*.
[27] He who earnestly seeks good finds favor,
But trouble will come to him who seeks *evil*.
[28] He who trusts in his riches will fall,
But the righteous will flourish like foliage.
[29] He who troubles his own house will inherit the wind,
And the fool *will be* servant to the wise of heart.
[30] The fruit of the righteous *is a* tree of life,
And he who wins souls *is* wise.

[31] If the righteous will be recompensed on the earth,
How much more the ungodly and the sinner.

The words of this passage stirred my heart and my eyes welled with joyful tears. As the tears rolled, I smiled and accepted the very special gift God had just given me. Through Proverbs 11, He showed me my spiritual makeover. I marveled at the contrast in each verse. I saw two opposing pictures of me. In one picture there was the distrustful and guarded woman who refused to surrender to the will of anyone, even God. In the other, a lovely picture of a morally strong woman who now is determined to reflect the qualities of a true believer.

Because of my past ugliness, I wondered if I had ever kept another person from conversion to Christianity or a deeper spiritual relationship with the Lord. In my earlier days, I was judgmental, rude and filled with pride. Now I am amazed at how much God has transformed my heart!

Then one day, I started to wonder if perhaps other Christians in the world carried shame from their own behavior and truly desired a more godly life. I immediately prayed and instantly felt an overwhelming need to tell my story.

This book is written for anyone struggling with questions about what the bible has to offer when pain, suffering and confusion have overshadowed feelings of love and grace. My life is a testimony of the loving hope I found through Jesus Christ. I am living proof that people can change!

CHAPTER THREE

I LEARNED THE VALUE OF CONFESSING MY SINS TO GOD

Proverbs 28:13 He who covers his sins will not prosper, But whoever confesses and forsakes them will have mercy (NKJV).

The meaning of this verse is very true for me. God has blessed me as I have examined my heart, become vulnerable and confessed my sins. I can also say with certainty, I was foolish to deny my sinfulness, and excuse it. When I covered my sins, I couldn't find true peace. But since beginning to humbly confess my sins, with true repentance and faith, I have found mercy from God. Therefore, I have no reservations in scrutinizing the Christian I was claiming to be and the one I am in the process of becoming and noting the bold differences between them.

Being raised in the Catholic Church, I had memorized, from an early age, a prayer of confession. Each week during mass, I would join the rest of the congregation in saying, "I confess to almighty God, and to you, my brothers and sisters, that I have sinned through my own fault, in my thoughts and in my words, in what I have done, and in what I have failed to do; and I ask Blessed Mary, ever virgin, all the angels and saints, and you, my brothers and sisters, to pray for me to the Lord our God." Further, I participated in confessing my sins to the priest in our congregation at least once a year, usually one week before Easter service. When I felt guilty as a young child for my behavior, such as sassing my mother, or lying, I would quickly confess my sins to God.

As I grew older, however, and my pride, arrogance and controlling attitude ruled my heart, I felt less of a need to confess my sins to God. At the time, I didn't realize how much my choice to sin separated me from God. In fact, over the period of many years, I had become so sinful that God's words no longer had any impact on my heart.

In October 2008, God offered me an opportunity to receive His grace and forgiveness. This time, my eyes opened to see how much I needed God. Then a few months later, I began bible classes to study God. In one school assignment, I reviewed several bible tracts. One particular tract grabbed my heart. The tract pictured a man on one side of a canyon and God on the other. Written across the canyon was the word, "Sin." I stared at that picture for quite awhile. The same week, in another class, I learned how God cannot tolerate the presence of sin. I began to admit, I am a sinner! I realized how distant from God I had chosen to roam. For much of my life, I committed offenses against God. And, I couldn't wait to change! I craved a renewed relationship with God and was willing to do whatever He asked to reunify with Him. I deeply and sincerely wanted His forgiveness.

I began to pray. At first, I only prayed in private. The first time, I found myself repeating the confessional prayer I learned as a child. I walked away unchanged. The next time, I prayed from my heart. I felt a sense of healing. God wanted to hear "I'm sorry," from my humbled heart. From then on, I was specific in my prayer while confessing my sin. I told God, as a child would tell her parent, what I did. Each time, I acknowledged that I was a sinner; I felt the warmth of God's forgiveness.

As I grew closer to God, I felt a burden to clear the past and confess my sins to others. I started by admitting to friends that I had not been the perfect wife or the Christian I had claimed to be. I was surprised at the response from my friends. In each conversation, my friends admitted their faults and failures too. It felt as if I had, at last, opened a door for truth to be spoken in love.

As a result, I heard about the many challenges and disappointments my friends' faced in their own marriages, parenting their children and at work. I no longer felt alone in my sadness. And I no longer felt the need to put on an outward show. I could finally be real!

I confessed to my friends how broken I was and how much I needed God. My friends shared with me how they had admired me for years and were relieved to know my life was not picture perfect. These conversations prompted me to speak God's name freely. Now, I could easily testify to His goodness and His ability to purify my heart.

Confessing my sins to my friends was very positive, so I then began the process with family members. As with friends, confessing my sins to family members offered healing by clearing up many misunderstandings and past hurts. I now believe that confession is another form of ministering to others. It creates a safe environment to start discussions about specific needs. It also allows me to pray for friends and family on a very personal level.

Additionally, confession brought a feeling of holiness and closeness to Christ. It also kept me accountable. Finally, confessing my sins taught me humility. I no longer exalt myself over another. And I am reminded daily that, yet born a sinner, there is forgiveness and deep abiding joy in God.

Joy Unspeakable
Text: Barney E. Warren, 1900
Music: Barney E. Warren, 1900

I have found His grace is all complete,
He supplieth ev'ry need;
While I sit and learn at Jesus' feet,
I am free, yes, free indeed.

I have found the pleasure I once craved,
It is joy and peace within;
What a wondrous blessing! I am saved
From the awful gulf of sin.

I have found that hope so bright and clear,
Living in the realm of grace;
Oh, the Savior's presence is so near,
I can see His smiling face.

I have found the joy no tongue can tell,
How its waves of glory roll!
It is like a great o'er flowing well,
Springing up within my soul.

CHAPTER FOUR

FROM UNDESERVING TO GRATEFUL; MY APOLOGY TO GOD

2 Chronicles 7:14. If my people, who are called by My name will humble themselves, and pray and seek My face, and turn from their wicked ways, then I will hear from heaven, and will forgive their sin, and heal their land (NKJV).

I have written this book to admit my sins and as my prayer to God asking forgiveness. I hope to demonstrate my desire to continually seek God and to express my longing to turn from my past sinful behavior. I am also writing to worship God and praise

Him. I wish to thank God for the many changes He has made in me and for the opportunities He has given me to surrender my life to Him. When I speak to God now through a repentant and humble heart, I say "I am truly sorry it took me so long to devote my life to Your will God, please forgive me! Thank You for sacrificing Your only Son for me. I love you!"

The night I was arrested, and a few months after, I found myself complaining about my life. I told others, "I didn't deserve what happened to me!" I felt sorry for myself and whined a lot. I grumbled about the handcuffs which had dug into my wrists and how I couldn't feel my thumbs for about two weeks. I talked about a painful seven inch bruise across my lower back. I told others I was embarrassed to be charged with a felony by the court system. In many conversations, I looked to others for sympathy.

However, since then, I have developed a completely different perspective regarding my arrest. These days, I stand in awe of God's faithfulness. I wonder why our God, creator of heaven and earth, gave me another opportunity to change my life. I still cannot grasp why He loves *me* so much.

Before celebrating Easter in 2009, I enrolled in a class called, <u>An Introduction to the New Testament</u>. Reading the Word was still very new to me. Continuously I picked up the bible, read a few verses, then put it down again. I was surprised at how much effort and time it was taking to understand the meaning of a few verses. I had a lot to learn!

As I read, I was troubled. It would be Easter and something was stirring my heart to understand Jesus' death and resurrection. Yet, as many times as I read the words, the meaning seemed to fall on deaf ears. I didn't understand!

In the past, I had successfully learned information by watching movies. So, I decided to rent a movie I hoped would portray the gospel of Christ's death and resurrection. Three years prior, the movie, *The Passion of the Christ,* by Mel Gibson was released. Despite its popularity, I had not yet seen the movie, so I rented the movie from the library. However, after only one scene, I was wet with tears. I quickly turned the DVD player off and placed the movie back in its sleeve. I just couldn't watch Jesus suffer. I was solemn for weeks.

When I returned to my assigned reading, I struggled again and I prayed for God's help. My youngest son interrupted my studies and asked me if he could watch a movie. Being a single mom at the time, I often sat him down to watch television so I could study. I browsed his DVD collection and found a cartoon video called *Worthy is the Lamb* by NEST Family Entertainment. Together we watched The Passion of the Christ in a simple cartoon format. I was starting to understand Christ's final hours and the blessing of his resurrection. I thought about the worst day of my life weighed against the worst day of the life of Jesus Christ. I compared each aspect and felt heaviness in my chest. The night Jesus was arrested he was abandoned by His friends. In His agony, He was left alone. The night I was arrested, God rushed family and friends to my side to console me.

Jesus suffered accusation by a whole multitude. My husband stood alone in his accusation against me.

Jesus' trial was travesty. My case never even made it to trial. Instead, the charges were quickly dismissed through a hearing held in an official courtroom with a lawyer who advocated for my innocence.

Jesus suffered humiliation from others who spat on Him and mocked Him. I was shown great compassion by a jail officer who sweetly said, "You are going to get through this."

Jesus' back was marred with lashings, while I only felt one bruise on my back.

From the large, ugly Roman nails, Jesus suffered permanent wounds to His hands, while I simply felt numbness in my thumbs for a couple of weeks.

Soldiers divided Jesus' garments and cast lots, while I was offered blankets to warm me.

Jesus carried the emotional weight of all of my sins on his shoulders. I didn't even recognize I was a sinner before my arrest. In His innocence, Jesus suffered. In my guilt, I was shown great mercy!

I am amazed at how much God loves me! One day, I began to think, "Why was I forgiven when Jesus was condemned? I am the sinner. I am nothing. Why does God even love me at all?" I had known about the choice to accept God's only Son, Jesus Christ, into my heart from an early age and I was too proud to receive this gift. Sadly, it took a great fall for me to finally reach up for help. Even so, God was there to pick me up and offer the gift of His Son once again. The feeling of gratitude towards God in sparing me the consequences I truly deserved overwhelms me. Yet, He continually affirms His love for me.

One day, while sitting in church, I drew a happy face on my five-year-old son's hand. Under the happy face, I wrote, "Hi." When I was finished, he smiled. He asked to use my pen. He then placed my hand in his lap and began to draw on the top of my hand. I glanced down and noticed my son was drawing a similar happy face. I figured he would write, "Hi mommy," on my hand. However, under the picture of the happy face, were the words, "God loves you." My eyes filled with tears. I said under my breath, "I love you too, God!"

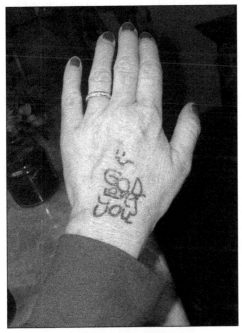

My son's drawing.

On another occasion, when I was thinking about how much God loves me, I came across a love letter called *"Father's love letter."* The letter was signed, "Love, Your Dad, Almighty God." I began to read the letter.

My Child,

You may not know me, but I know everything about you (Psalm 139:1). I know when you sit down and when you rise up (Psalm 139:2). I am familiar with all your ways (Psalm 139:3). Even the very hairs on your head are numbered (Matthew 10:29-31). For you were made in my image (Genesis 1:27). In me you live and move and have your being (Acts 17:28). For you are my offspring (Acts 17:28). I knew you even before you were conceived (Jeremiah 1:4-5). I chose you when I planned creation (Ephesians 1:11-12). You were not a mistake, for all your days are written in my book (Psalm 139:15-16). I determined the exact time of your birth and where you would live (Acts 17:26). You are fearfully and wonderfully made (Psalm 139:14). I knit you together in your mother's womb (Psalm 139:13). And brought you forth on the day you were born (Psalm 71:6). I have been misrepresented by those who don't know me (John 8:41-44). I am not distant and angry, but am the complete expression of love (1 John 4:16). And it is my desire to lavish my love on you (1 John 3:10). Simply because you are my child and I am your Father (1 John 3:1).

I offer you more than your earthly father ever could (Matthew 7:11). For I am the perfect father

(Matthew 5:48). Every good gift that you receive comes from my hand (James 1:17). For I am your provider and I meet all your needs (Matthew 6:31-33). My plan for your future has always been filled with hope (Jeremiah 29:11). Because I love you with an everlasting love (Jeremiah 31:3).

My thoughts toward you are countless as the sand on the seashore (Psalms 139:17-18). And I rejoice over you with singing (Zephaniah 3:17). I will never stop doing good for you (Jeremiah 32:40). For you are my treasured possession (Exodus 19:5). I desire to establish you with all my heart and all my soul (Jeremiah 32:41). And I want to show you great and marvelous things (Jeremiah 33:3). If you seek me with all your heart, you will find me (Deuteronomy 4:29). Delight in me and I will give you the desires of your heart (Psalm 37:4). For it is I who gave you those desires (Philippians 2:13). I am able to do more for you than you could possibly imagine (Ephesians 3:20). For I am your greatest encourager (2 Thessalonians 2:16-17). I am also the Father who comforts you in all your troubles (2 Corinthians 1:3-4). When you are brokenhearted, I am close to you

(Psalm 34:18). As a shepherd carries a lamb, I have carried you close to my heart

(Isaiah 40:11). One day I will wipe away every tear from your eyes (Revelation 21:3-4). And I'll take away all the pain you have suffered on this earth. (Revelation 21:3-4).

I am your Father, and I love you even as I love my son, Jesus (John 17:23). For in Jesus, my love for you is revealed (John 17:26). He is the exact

35

representation of my being (Hebrews 1:3). He came to demonstrate that I am for you, not against you (Romans 8:31). And to tell you that I am not counting your sins (2 Corinthians 5:18-19). Jesus died so that you and I could be reconciled (2 Corinthians 5:18-19). His death was the ultimate expression of my love for you (1 John 4:10). I gave up everything I loved that I might gain your love (Romans 8:31-32). If you receive the gift of my son Jesus, you receive me (1 John 2:23). And nothing will ever separate you from my love again (Romans 8:38-39). Come home and I'll throw the biggest party heaven has ever seen (Luke 15:7).

I have always been Father, and will always be Father (Ephesians 3:14-15). My question is…Will you be my child (John 1:12-13)? I am waiting for you (Luke 15:11-32).

Love, Your Dad
Almighty God

Father's Love Letter used by permission Father Heart Communications Copyright 1999-2010 www.FathersLoveLetter.com

I never knew how much God loved me until I surrendered my life to Him. In that moment, with my head hung low, He poured out His love for me. He did everything He said He would do. God kept His promises to me. He knew me before I was born and waited patiently for me to accept His love. I have written a letter to God in return.

Holy and Forgiving Father,

I may not know everything about You, but I am trying to learn. I am becoming familiar with Your ways. Thank You for creating me in Your image. Thank You for writing my name in Your book. I am sorry that I misrepresented You because I didn't know You. I know now, You are the complete expression of love and it is my only desire to worship You. Thank You for every gift You have provided to me from Your own hand. I know now You will meet all of my needs and Your plan for my future is filled with hope. I stand in awe of Your countless thoughts toward me. I think of You continuously too! I praise You with singing.

Thank You for calling me Your treasured child. With all my heart and all my soul, I desire to establish a relationship with Your only Son, Jesus Christ. I want to make You proud. I adore You with all my heart and have found delight in You. You have done more for me than I could possibly imagine and have been my greatest encourager. You have comforted me in all my troubles. When I was brokenhearted, You drew me near. You dried the tears from my eyes and healed my pain.

Thank you Father for loving me as You love Your son, Jesus. Thank You for not counting my sins. I would give up everything as I return Your love. I have received the gift of Your son Jesus- nothing will ever separate me from Your love again. I wait in joyful hope of going home to You. I love you God!

Love,
    Your daughter, Donna

God's love is Amazing! I have never experienced the intense love I have in my heart for God through any earthly relationship. Every day, I am excited and have a growing sense of completeness as I know Him more. I pour my heart out to God and He returns my love. A simple apology doesn't seem enough. I am grateful for the gift of His son, Jesus. Thank you God for your Amazing Love. I am sorry I didn't return your love sooner. I deeply and sorrowfully apologize for the wasted years I spent making my life about everything but You. Please forgive me God!

CHAPTER FIVE

A CHRISTIAN BY NAME ONLY

Proverbs 11:3 The integrity of the upright will guide them, But the perversity of the unfaithfulwill destroy them (NKJV).

Even though I called myself a Christian, I didn't become a true Christian until age thirty eight. Up until that time, I rarely walked with integrity and had not surrendered my life to Jesus Christ. By leading a dishonest life filled with unfaithfulness to my heavenly father, I caused myself years of unnecessary misery and pain. Once I submitted my life to Christ and began to lead an honest life, I found direction and guidance.

As a teenager, my behavior was quite contradictory to my profession of faith. In my heart, I knew I was walking away, day by day, from the light of Christ. I mastered the art of rationalization and at times even had myself fooled. I told others that I loved the Lord, but I was acting otherwise-drinking, partying and doing anything else that gained attention. It was easy to sway me one way or the other if it meant I gained approval from others.

By the time I met my husband, I had been steadily moving down a path of destruction and sin for years. The pattern was set. While I attended church each week and worked for Christian based employers, it was in my private life, where I surrounded myself with people who gave themselves to sin and were content with that life. I frequented a country western bar to pursue my ideal husband, a "Christian Cowboy." I met my husband exactly where I was looking for him- in a bar.

The night we met, he was almost too drunk to stand up. We met when his Navy buddy and the girl friend I was with sought to dance with each other. My now husband and I were invited to dance on the floor with them. During our dance, the conversation turned personal as he told me he was in the middle of a divorce and about how he had just returned from the war in Iraq. I felt immediate compassion for his situation with his wife. However, I judged him as an unsuitable partner for me based on his excessive drinking, his failed marriage and the fact that he already had children. It also bothered me that he was enlisted in the military. My mother had convinced me that the military life was not for me. My biological father served in the Air Force and my mother spoke negatively about her experience as a military wife. Because of her stories, I swore never to marry someone serving in the military. Also, I wanted a partner who did not have other children and who desired at least one with me.

I shared with this man that I had called off my own second engagement just weeks prior and even had the *white* dress still hanging on my bedroom door. I spoke about how I was trying to save face with friends and family as I returned wedding presents.

During this conversation, we decided that we weren't right for each other. Yet as strangers, we expressed compassion for the pain we were both experiencing. I said to the Navy man as we slow danced, "I am sorry that your wife cheated on you and hurt your son." He quickly replied, "I am sorry you were hurt too." I could see how alone and vulnerable he felt and my heart opened to him.

Today, I think about the dancing we shared. Was God opening the door to a relationship filled with compassion? In my blindness and skewed Christian walk, had I sadly focused on this man's shortcomings rather than the loving-kindness he was offering?

I wonder if I was the Christian then that I am today, if I would have taken that moment to share with this broken man how much God loves him. All judgments aside, I could have told this man that he was not alone. I could have offered him hope through scripture or confirmed that we can't always know why things happen but that they happen to bring glory to God.

At the time of our dance, however, the path of my Christian walk was not straight. I communicated mercy the best that I knew how to do that evening. As the night progressed, I watched the man dance with other women. He was acting ridiculously immature in my eyes so I avoided him and danced with another gentleman who had caught my eye earlier. As we left, my girl friend and the Navy man's friend struck up a conversation outside the bar. Left to stare at each other, the navy man and I resumed talking. He was sobering up. I told him, "My name is Donna," and he replied, "My name is LeeRoy." After we introduced ourselves properly we continued to talk. We realized we had much in common. We especially talked about our love for motorcycles. So that night, I gave LeeRoy my phone number. He called the next day and we spoke at length on the phone. I agreed to a date with him on a motorcycle ride.

Surprised at my appearance, as I opened the door on our first date, he said, "Wow, you are pretty!" Apparently, LeeRoy was too drunk to see what I looked like the night we met. I remember thinking on that day, "Oh, well, we can still be friends."

We rode his motorcycle regularly for the next few months. It became our courting ritual. He began to visit me at work, and on one occasion, brought his son. I fell instantly in love with LeeRoy's son. I also met his daughter during the first few months, their mother and LeeRoy's parents. Each person in his family quickly left a positive impression on me.

Our dating experience was filled with laughter and entertainment. We went to a fireworks show during our summer romance, and for the first and only time in my life, I saw heart shaped fireworks light up the sky. We drove to Magic Mountain, swam in the pool, walked on the beach and rode the motorcycle. It was very romantic. Our romance became a beautiful distraction for both of our pain. I still attended church, but my behavior was contradictory to my Christian beliefs. It was very worldly. I invited LeeRoy to attend church with me one Sunday and he agreed. It only took him one service to decide church was not for him. Because of his many negative comments, I did not ask again.

After a few months of dating, I discovered LeeRoy had a tender heart and my feelings began to change. He continued to allow his vulnerable side to shine through his tough exterior. In one conversation, LeeRoy told me about the loss of his first son who died at the age of 2 ½ to a congenital defect called Spinal bifida. He talked about being a teenager at the time of his son's death. We cried together when he spoke of the profound emotional effect the loss had on him. He also talked of his failed marriage. I heard his side of the story. I admired his ability to overcome adversity. I began to think about a future with him. Perhaps I really loved him. So when LeeRoy responded positively to the question of having more children, I started to push for my third engagement. We became engaged.

LeeRoy was still active duty when he asked me to marry him. We lived forty miles apart and I was with him at his home many hours each day. For several reasons, I moved in with LeeRoy prior to the wedding and before his divorce was finalized. We slept together and began drinking alcohol regularly. I ignored my conscious mind when it told me to stop and think about the choices I was making.

Everything, including the movies we watched was on display for his fourteen year-old-son and eight year-old-daughter. I set an example for these children as well as my thirteen-year-old niece who spent time with us. As a woman of God, I devalued myself in many ways.

My fiancé agreed with whatever I asked him to do and was very eager to please me. I wanted to please him too. I thought I was compromising by watching his choice of movies which often portrayed violence and sexual content. There were times when I stood up for my values, but they were infrequent and random. I requested that we meet with the base chaplain for premarital counseling to prepare for our marriage. He complied. However, on several occasions after praying with the Chaplain, we would resume watching his choice of television shows. Even though I wanted God to rule my life, Satan ruled my home.

Once married, God was no longer allowed in our home by my husband. The inability to discuss church, Christ and God made me more judgmental and self-righteous. In our home, I ruled out all drinking, violent content on the television and hanging out in bars: literally, the war began. If LeeRoy didn't agree with my new changes, I'd react and be mean. I would manipulate, pick on his son, argue, slander him for his past, belittle his education, and gossip about him to my family and friends. He then would retaliate and attack verbally, financially and emotionally. He often attacked me spiritually by demeaning God, church and by pointing out my hypocrisy.

Merely bringing up God or asking for prayer increased attacks between us. I couldn't see at the time *whom* I was fighting against. I thought I was in control of my marriage and our situation. But the more I tried to control, the more powerless I felt.

Throughout these months, I prayed as if I had faith. I attended the base chapel and required my husband and children accompany me. They begrudgingly went for Easter and Christmas services.

With little understanding of God's values for marriage, I was determined to be the law in my home. I attempted through threats, guilt and manipulation to lead my new family to Christ. None of my ways worked!

It was my behavior during our courtship and engagement that set an example which my new family expected to continue. For nine months, sinfulness and my attitude of "everything goes" was the way of life. I had given my husband priority over God and sin over righteousness. I didn't understand that my forcefulness towards my new family to love Christ was actually pushing them away. I neglected to comprehend how confusing and incredibly difficult it is for contemporary society to discuss and even accept Christ. How foreign the concept of God was to my new family! My own guilt gripped me and as a wife I was throwing the entire blame on my husband. Sadly, my life was void of a strong godly foundation and I was living my life allowing Satan to overtake me, not God.

I spent much of my early marriage relying on myself for answers. I did not turn to the Lord for guidance, support and forgiveness. As a result, my life was misdirected and very depressing. My marriage was unhealthy and I was setting a poor example as a Christian.

In late 2008, I finally told God He was first in my life. Next, I started conversations with my husband about my sincere desire for real faith. I prayed for and with LeeRoy. Surprisingly, one night almost a year later, LeeRoy mentioned he wanted to go to church with me. The service was shorter than usual and less church members attended that night. The associate pastor was methodically teaching in the book of Philippians. My husband liked the service and began to attend church weekly. As God would have it, the message we heard every Wednesday night for months was "press on, fight the good fight." Through Scripture, we were encouraged to practice humility in our relationship with one another (Philippians 2:5-11). We learned about the road to spiritual maturity and to *press on* toward the goal which Christ called us to (Philippians 3:12-16). We began to look forward to our future and to leave our past failures behind. We began to imitate Paul's attitude. As a result, for the first time in our turbulent marriage, we were holding hands in church. We both spoke about the peace and enjoyment we felt sitting in that back pew by each others' side. I often found myself in tears as I heard us turn the pages of our bibles together.

After a church service one night, I heard a song by Josh Wilson called, *Before the Morning*. The song confirmed the message we heard for months in church, "*There is good for those who love God.*" The conscious decision we made to leave our old marriage behind and start over with like-mindedness in Christ transformed our marriage. Over time, the compassion we felt while dating returned and our marriage became stronger and more loving than we could ever had imagined.

Today, LeeRoy and I are seriously considering repeating our marriage vows. This time we plan on inviting Jesus Christ to the ceremony. Each day, we turn to Christ for guidance in our marriage. For the first time, I am happily married and cherish the moments I share with my husband.

We spent a day together recently that I will not soon forget. Last year, my husband had to sell his motorcycle to afford to pay his taxes. I was sad to see him sell his bike. So, as a present for Father's day, I surprised LeeRoy with a gift certificate from a Harley dealership. The certificate allowed my husband to rent a motorcycle for one day. I was pleasantly surprised when he asked to take me for a ride. On the Harley, we rode through the same canyons as on our first date.

At first, my husband drove under the speed limit. It was very hot outside that day. While he drove slowly, I rode with the face screen in the up position. The Harley we rented came with a radio which my husband immediately tuned to a local Country station. With my face screen up, I could hear the music playing from the motorcycle. I listened as an older country song played. The artist, sang, "Heaven only knows how I've been blessed with the gift of your love... Oh Lord I'd be lost, but for the grace of God."

The words penetrated my heart. Streams of tears began to role down my cheeks. I looked up to the heavens and thanked God. I shook my head as I realized I had finally fallen in love with my husband and it was *because* of all that had happened between us. While saying this little prayer, I realized the crisis from October 2008 was now behind us. All had been forgiven!

To my husband, I ask your forgiveness for all the years I led you away from a true relationship with Christ. I am sorry for the example I set and for those times I judged you without mercy. Please forgive me!

Harley Ride 2010

CHAPTER SIX

FROM EVIL WORDS TO WISE DISCERNMENT

Proverbs 11:9 The hypocrite with his mouth destroys his neighbor, But through knowledge the righteous will be delivered (NKJV).

My evil and hasty words destroyed my friends and family. And a result I often felt a frailty of spirit, guilt, depression and shame. In October 2008, I surrendered my life to God. As a result, He offered me fellowship with the Holy Spirit, the comfort of His arms, a rock to lean upon and wise discernment.

When we first met, my mother-in-law was kind to me. She was staying with my husband then. Each time I visited his home, we became more acquainted. She talked about my husband's upbringing and about her tragic divorce to his father after thirty years of marriage. Since, I had never been married, or been in a relationship which lasted for more than three years, I couldn't relate to the commitment and heartbreak she described. It had been years since she had contact with my husband's father and she had no desire to resume connection. Within a few months of the courtship with my husband, my mother-in-law returned to her home in England.

When my husband asked me to marry him, I immediately started the guest list. I couldn't imagine not inviting his mother. I called her and asked her to attend. She came. From my perspective, the wedding turned out to be very beautiful. I was grateful both LeeRoy's parents attended without fuss. At the time, I didn't consider my mother-in-law's sacrifice to fly from another country or how uncomfortable she must have felt seeing my husband's father again.

Then, approximately three years after our marriage ceremony, my husband retired from service in the military. I wanted my mother-in-law to attend my husband's retirement ceremony. My husband was convinced she would not attend. One day, I called my mother-in-law, told her about the retirement ceremony and invited her. She politely refused. But I couldn't accept her negative response, so I begged her to come. She reluctantly got on another plane and came a second time.

As the retirement approached, I began to feel overwhelmed. I was parenting a teenage stepson and a toddler while working full-time. After work, my husband went to the golf course on base. The caring of our home and children was left for me to handle. I was excited when my mother-in-law arrived. Someone to talk to! I told her about the discord between my husband and me. Surprisingly, she was empathetic. Lovingly, she offered to care for my young son while my husband and I enjoyed a night out together. However, I was too afraid to let go of control of my family.

Over the next week, tension built up between my husband and his mother and my husband and me. Trying to play mediator between my husband and his mother and keep everyone "happy" consumed me. I blamed my mother-in-law for the extra tension in our home. Without consulting my husband, I confronted her. Hastily, I conveyed the message that she was no longer welcome. My mother-in-law left our home that same day and refused subsequent contact with me.

Like so many times before, I tried to clean up my mess. I wrote to her and bought her gifts for her birthday and Mother's Day. One day while she was on the phone with my husband, I begged him to let me speak to her. We spoke for the first time in years. However, rather than admitting I had hurt her, I simply justified my actions. My mother-in-law deserved a humble apology. But I was too proud to show her Christ.

God has since burdened my heart about my misplaced anger and hasty words which hurt my mother-in-law so many years ago. Consequently, I began to pray for her. I also recently asked God to show me our relationship through my mother-in-laws eyes.

God responded. One day our family drove to play in the snow. On the way, I reread this chapter. My bible was under the manuscript on my lap. The bible slipped to the side of my lap and an old prayer card fell from it. Written on the card was the prayer of St. Francis of Assisi. I read the prayer, "Lord, make me an instrument of your peace. Where there is hatred, let me sow love. Where there is injury, pardon. Where there is doubt, faith. Where there is despair, hope. Where there is darkness, light. Where there is sadness, joy. O Divine Master, grant that I may not so much seek to be consoled, as to console. To be understood, as to understand. To be loved, as to love. For it is in giving that we receive. It is in pardoning that we are pardoned. It is in dying that we are born to eternal life." -St. Francis of Assisi.

I again thought about my relationship with my mother-in-law. I felt warmth return to my heart for my mother-in-law. I wondered what our relationship would be like today, had I embraced this prayer during our last encounter. For years, during mass in the Catholic Church, I sang these words. I realized I had sung them in vain. God deliberately placed a Christian in my mother-in-laws life. But I misrepresented Him. Had I failed God?

During that last visit, my mother-in-law was clearly upset. I didn't offer her peace. She spoke the hatred in her heart. I didn't sow love. Even when I was to blame for hurting her feelings, I didn't ask forgiveness. In her darkness, I didn't show light and in her sadness, I didn't spread joy. By His plan, God placed me in a broken family of unbelievers. I had an opportunity to bring them to the arms of Jesus Christ. I was too sinful to respond to God's call.

Another mother who deserves an apology is my own. Though my mother-in-law and I are just beginning to know each other, my own mother has been a stable force throughout my life. Even such, I have said hurtful things to my own mother as well. Looking back now, I realize how as a child I directed my anger at the parent I relied on the most. I told my mother, "I hate you" when I was angry. As an adult, I gossiped about my mother when she said something that stabbed my heart.

Yet, I called my mother the night I was arrested. She drove two and a half hours, put $5,000.00 on her credit card and paid my bail. She even humbled herself before the man who had just physically hurt me to request that he release my youngest son to her care. My mother must have suffered through it all. Still, she never asked for anything in return.

My mother was dependable my entire life. During my childhood, she worked standing on her feet for long hours to support my sister and me. She gave of herself altruistically to family and friends. She loved the Lord and her family. She maintained a stable marriage for over twenty-five years with my stepfather, whom I now call "dad," and "friend." As a teenager, growing up, my years were up and down and I felt angry and confused. As a result, my words towards my mother were often mean-out of haste and rage.

I pondered over writing this chapter for months. Often I was filled with regret for my past behavior towards both my mother and mother-in-law. I wasn't sure how to even begin writing this chapter. While writing, I felt the pain I caused and cried. We are commanded by God to honor our parents. With wicked words, I failed God. I stopped many times to feel deep remorse and ask God for forgiveness.

Then one day, when I was feeling the heavy weight of who I had been, a song played on the radio. Soon I was tearing up again as the words flowed through me. The artist sang about the devil's ability to remind us of our past failures and wrongs. I heard my feelings being sung out loud. Then suddenly he sang, "I know what I've been, but here in your arms, I know what I am, I'm forgiven!" Incredible! I knew God had forgiven me, now I needed to forgive myself. I immediately started to pray for my mother-in-law. I asked God to intercede and please bring a joyful and loving Christian into her life. Perhaps in the future, the person He will send will be the repentant me.

I know when I next speak with my mother-in-law; I will respectfully apologize for my behavior and ask for her forgiveness. Then, I will humbly ask God for strength to be an example of His love, compassion and mercy to my mother-in-law in all future communication.

I also pray for my own mother. However, for her, my prayers are of thanksgiving to God for the mother He chose for me. I thank God for her heart towards her children. Thank you Mom, you always let me run to you for help. And thank you Mom, for your willingness to rescue me in times of need. I ask for forgiveness for my harsh words, and want to express my extreme gratitude.

To both my mother and my mother-in-law, I say, "I am sorry. Please forgive me."

CHAPTER SEVEN

FROM JUDGMENTAL
TO MERCIFUL

Proverbs 11:17 The merciful man does good for his own soul, But *he who* is cruel troubles his own flesh (NKJV).

In the past, I was mean to others. I often judged people harshly and formed immediate opinions. I rarely showed others mercy. I held grudges. I was even told once "You are mean!" I didn't realize then, that my abrasive behavior towards others was hurting my own soul.

One of the greatest blessings from my experience in October 2008 was a 7-day restraining order from the court system. Because I was charged with physical violence against my husband, the sheriff's deputies requested that the Judge grant a restraining order. The order legally kept me from seeing or speaking to my husband and our under-aged son. While I grieved the absence of my 3-year-old son for 7 days, I also became friends with my sister for the first time.

I couldn't return to my home where my husband and child were living after my release from jail. Therefore, I had to find a place to stay for a week. I called my sister and asked if I could sleep on her couch while my mother implored my husband to let our son stay with her until the order was released. It was humbling to ask my sister for help because we were not friends and I had been judgmental and critical of her my entire life. Unbelievably, my sister welcomed me to both her home and heart- no strings attached. She instantly offered me mercy and a lifetime of forgiveness. If I could picture Jesus welcoming me home after sinning against Him in my lifetime, it would be exactly in the same manner as my sister's open door. Each morning before work, she made hot tea for me and listened as I cried over my current situation. She owned a very large and intimidating bulldog that stretched out all over the couch I slept on. But even the dog was gentle and kind to me as he laid his head on my lap while I cried. My sister overwhelmed me with her grace and tremendous amount of compassion. Through her, I was learning to become merciful.

My only sister, older by a year, is a Christian in our Lord Jesus Christ and throughout her life has embraced one of the bible's most repeated commands, to love your neighbor as you love yourself.

During this difficult time in my life, she was kind even to me after many years of my ungratefulness.

My sister wasn't the only one I had harshly judged. Judging others was a regular habit for me. In 2000, I participated in a mission trip to Mombassa, Africa, and my travel companions were Mormon. Also at the time, I dated a man who was Jewish. I spoke my mind with misunderstood conviction to both my fellow missionaries and my boyfriend. I pressured my boyfriend to convert to Christianity and judged him when he refused. I really thought that I was being open-minded by dating someone who was Jewish and for serving God with Mormons, all of whom did not share the same religious philosophy as me.

Today, I feel regret for the way I judged others. I am particularly sorrowful when I recall how my sister and past boyfriend put up with a lot of my anger and embarrassing putdowns from me.

In the relationship with my Jewish boyfriend, I immediately interjected into our conversations hurtful comments and judgment. For example, it only took a week for me to tell him that he was "Going to Hell for not believing in Jesus." I remember watching his spirit break as I told him what I believed to be the Truth. Not only was my approach detrimental, but so was my inaccurate information. These days, the relationship I had with my past Jewish boyfriend holds a different meaning for me. I reflect on who I was over 15 years ago and how much my faith has grown in the past two years. With him, I observed Jewish Tradition. I had an opportunity to listen as he spoke in Hebrew. I keenly understand now how I missed a very special gift to be among God's chosen people and see Christ's heritage with my own eyes.

Further, it is agonizingly apparent to me that I was wrong about "my truth." In my arrogance and judgment all I accomplished was to provide further justification to my past Jewish boyfriend not to convert to Christianity. If I were to see my past Jewish boyfriend today, I would say, "I am sorry, please forgive me, not all Christians behave like I did when we dated." Then, knowing he speaks Hebrew, I would tell him, "Baruch Hashem Adoni," which means "Blessed be the name of the Lord."

By the grace of God, the experience with my husband bonded me with my sister. She has begun to share her life with me and we have started calling each other "friend." To my sister whom I judged without mercy for so many years, I am sorry and I ask for your forgiveness. Thank you for teaching me how to be merciful. Thank you for your compassion during one of my greatest trials in life and everyday since.

My sister and me.

CHAPTER EIGHT

FROM BITTER HEART TO PURE HEART

Proverbs 11:20 Those who are of a perverse heart are an abomination to the LORD, But the blameless in their ways are His delight (NKJV).

For the sake of clarity in this book, I will refer to my husband's son as my stepson. However, in reality, I simply call him "Son."

I entered my stepson's life only a few years after his mother and father's divorce. Almost immediately, I felt a connection to him. He was a cute teenager with bleached out, blonde hair. He wore braces and a lovable smile. He often entertained me and was quick to compliment me. During those first few months, my stepson and I remained mannerly. We seemed to get along well. One day, he let his guard down. Perhaps, he felt he could trust me with his true emotions. I started to regularly observe feelings such as sorrow, frustration, and guilt. I recognized how brokenhearted he was and how he looked to me for guidance. At the time, I was spiritually immature and self-righteous. I arrogantly declared, "I'm an experienced Social Worker and an expert in working with troubled teens (like him)." I realize now, I missed an opportunity to provide hope by telling my stepson about the healing power of Jesus Christ.

Instead, I developed a habit of regularly calling attention to my stepson's difficulties. Simultaneously, I wore a cross around my neck and emphasized my own morality. I presented a holier-than-thou attitude. Without a doubt, my behavior most likely caused him to think, "If that is what a Christian is, I don't want to be one!"

Once, my stepson, then fifteen, tried to confront me regarding my conduct. He told me that none of his friends wanted to spend time in our home because of me. He didn't explain why, but I wouldn't have listened anyway. I responded to his accusation by rationalizing that his friends were using drugs and didn't want to be called on their behavior. He didn't know Jesus Christ at the time, and I was telling him to make new friends, Christian friends. I wanted him to act like a Christian, a Christian like me. I was ignorant to my own behavior.

In 2010, as a birthday gift, I asked my husband for a machine which converts Video Home System

(VHS) tapes to digital versatile discs (DVDs). I wanted to make home DVDs as Christmas gifts for family members. I didn't realize until I received the present, how much of a blessing this machine would become. The converter allowed me to watch old family tapes as the footage recorded onto DVD. As I watched our family have fun at the beach, lake and Disneyland, I remembered a verse, Proverbs 11:20. God was about to reveal to me my past behavior.

In the tapes, I heard myself belittling my children and husband with my harsh tone and sarcasm. I also heard myself make jokes which were often indecent and seemed to embarrass my older children. Because my stepson lived with us full-time, he witnessed the majority of these negative behaviors.

As I was watching these home family videos, I was able to see with my own eyes how critically I spoke about my stepson. I felt embarrassment and remorse for my words and actions. I really wanted to mute the sound button and at times simply turn the tapes off. In fact, after only an hour, I lost the desire to make copies for others. How could I let anyone have a permanent record of my past behavior on tape? It was tough to face the truth of who I was. However, I eventually continued to create the DVD's as Christmas gifts to keep the promise I made.

Making the tapes took days of effort, during which I thought about how I depended on my own under-standing to guide my family. I especially mulled over the example I set for my stepson. I considered how mean I was at times. As I looked back with regret on the pain I had caused him, I realized I hadn't lit the way for this child, nor did I teach him to show others compassion during their time of need. I felt heavy-hearted. I wondered if my stepson could ever forgive me. Then, as God would have it, I immediately recalled the week of October 20, 2008.

Two days after my arrest, my stepson appeared at my mother's home. He hadn't told his father he was coming and decided on his own to visit me. I thought he'd believe his father's lies and turn away from me. Instead, he came with mercy and compassion. He didn't belittle me for having issues with his father, nor did he use profanity or try to embarrass me. He simply opened his arms and hugged me. He continued to support me emotionally through the court proceedings. He never passed judgment or even asked for an explanation for what happened between his father and me. Through my stepson, God was leading *me* into a deeper relationship with Jesus Christ. And God was just starting to influence my heart.

In the weeks that followed, God continued to reach out to me. Just eleven days after being arrested came the holiday, Halloween. I used to love Halloween and participated in all of its activities. My parents, whom my son and I were still staying with, planned on celebrating the holiday. To my surprise, I suddenly saw Halloween as evil and demonic. I felt convicted to avoid Halloween altogether. Instead, I stayed at a hotel for the night with my youngest son. As I called for hotel reservations, I rethought my decision about not carving pumpkins and allowing my son to dress up. As God would have it, the children were going door to door early that night. The first few children were dressed in frightening masks and scared my youngest son with their costumes. I drove away from my mother's home feeling a sense of relief.

Next, I noticed my taste change toward my favorite television shows. Now programs portraying drinking or displaying a lot of violence, especially domestic violence, left me feeling nauseated. As a result, I stopped watching many of the popular dramas and sitcoms I used to love. Suddenly, I craved positive and Christ-centered material. I couldn't absorb enough documentaries about God, Jesus and His first followers. Negative past media images in my head were being replaced with biblical history. I felt my heart continue to heal!

Then God communicated with me through music. I moved into the new apartment to provide a safe place for my younger son. The apartment was small compared to our family home. Reception for a cellular phone and radio stations were limited in the area. I felt the effects of the poor radio reception right away and found myself listening to static when I tried to tune into my usual Country radio station. After a week, I became frustrated and began to tune through radio stations to find another with clearer reception.

One day, while moving the station dial back and forth, I came across a song which grabbed my attention immediately. I cried as God tugged on my heart. The artist sang, "I'm coming back to a heart of worship, and it's all about you, all about you Jesus." I sobbed as I knelt on my knees. I began to pray and apologize to God. I admitted that my life to that point had been about me. I had worshipped myself. My life was about how I wanted my house to be, how I wanted others to behave, how I expected to be treated and how I defined love. I was focused on myself, my needs and what pleased me. It was the first moment I realized God should have priority-even over my family. I decided to turn my life over to God and began to worship Him.

With the hopes of hearing the song again, I continued to listen to the station for the next few weeks. For the first time, I was listening to spiritual songs outside of a church choir. I was surprised at how much I enjoyed the songs that played. For years, I was under the impression that I was "too cool" to listen to Christian radio and that the songs were corny. Now, I was finding comfort in every song and beginning to feel uncomfortable with the songs I listened to in the past.

Around the same time, God led me to an internet site that streamed Christian music. I began downloading songs and playing them repeatedly. Each time, I cried as I heard artists sing about their lives and the words of scripture. I couldn't explain the sense of comfort and change I was going through, but God was reaching out to me through spiritual songs and my heart was softening.

I had begun my journey down the path towards refinement in God's eyes. For the first time in my life, I was becoming holy. By choosing God over worldly television shows, songs and activities that weren't about Him, I was transforming into the Christian God had planned for me. I was no longer a hypocrite.

This past year, I prayed for God to use the situation between my husband and me to bring my stepson into a relationship with his Son, Jesus Christ. He answered my prayer! In conversations, my stepson has begun to talk about God. He tells me stories of declaring his faith in Jesus Christ. God not only used the crisis in our family to change me but He also led my stepson through his own spiritual journey.

Today, I reminisce about those early years with my stepson. I flash back to times, remembering his innocence and pure heart. I thank God for my stepson's ability to forgive and love me despite my negative Christian example. I thank God for placing him in my life to teach me His ways. Through many tears, I beg God to continue to purify my own heart. I tell God, "I don't feel worthy to be used by You, but I am ready to try."

To my stepson, I now say, "I am sorry. Please forgive me for the ugly example I set as a Christian. Thank you for loving me anyway. From this point forward, I promise to be the holy and gracious mother-figure that you deserve. I am proud to call you my son and always will be."

CHAPTER NINE

FROM THE DISCOURAGING WORD TO THE HEALING WORD

**Proverbs 15:4-6 A wholesome
tongue is a tree of life,
But perverseness in it
breaks the spirit (NKJV).**

Prior to October 2008, I never understood the power of words. I didn't understand how a gentle word could encourage the soul or how a cruel word could devastate one's spirit. While living an unholy life, I used words to express my anger, to discourage and to control others. I have since discovered how words of the righteous can influence, support and even win souls.

Growing up, I was told to ignore others when they said thoughtless comments. I was raised to believe the saying, "Sticks and stones may break my bones, but words can never hurt me." Consequently, I learned that words didn't matter. Only when I sassed my mother, would she attempt to discipline my mouth. Despite her efforts, I kept those bad word habits. And, I spent much of my life expressing my own thoughtless opinions.

I had conversational bad habits too. I dominated dialogue between others and myself. I spoke a lot and listened very little. I interrupted others mid-sentence and practiced mind reading. I took no pleasure in listening to others. My main motive in speaking was to get attention. Words to me, served as "filler." They didn't mean anything. On October 20, 2008, I learned words are a powerful tool.

Approximately two hours before being booked in the county jail, I started a conversation with my husband. We had been fighting during the entire weekend. Tension was already high between us. I approached my husband hoping to end his silent treatment.

In the past, in order to communicate with my husband when he was angry, I had to take a lower physical posture and be the first to say, "I am sorry." So, on this night, I sat on the floor next to his favorite chair and looked up at him. In a soft tone, I said I was sorry and tried to explain that I was hurt by his behavior. He remained silent.

To get his attention, I shared my anxiety over my upcoming surgery to have all of my wisdom teeth removed. I had very little experience with anesthesia. While I spoke about the dangers of the surgery and all that could go wrong, my husband coldly stared at the ceiling with his arms crossed over his chest and had a scowl on his face. I was certain he wanted to "make up," so I persisted.

At the time, I didn't know he had taken a combination of several of his prescription medications. While we lived under the same roof, it was not uncommon for us to spend time in separate rooms.

I kept talking about my fears. Finally, my husband looked straight at me. He smiled an ear to ear grin and said, "It would be a *blessing* if something happened to you."

I immediately stopped talking. I was stunned! I sat back on my heals. His words and the look on his face pierced through my heart.

I thought about his choice of words. Because of his lack of experience with church or the bible, I was sure my husband didn't know the meaning of the word "blessing." I became defensive and angry. I took off my wedding ring, gave it to him and said, "I cannot do this anymore." By giving him back the ring, I knew I was starting a war.

In our battle of wills, words were our main weapon. Through the use of his words, my husband was convincing to the sheriff's deputies and caused my arrest. In an instant, I thought, "Maybe words really do matter."

I was still in great shock when the patrol car reached the jail. Once inside the double doors, the handcuffs were removed. I felt disoriented. I had to continually remind myself I was not dreaming. Even today, my booking into the jail remains foggy. I can't remember clearly which came first, the fingerprinting, the mug shot, or speaking with the bail bondsman on the phone. However, what I do remember distinctly about that night two years ago, were the words said by each person I had contact with. Their words and tone left a profound impression on my heart that still remains today.

It was calming to hear the tone of the jail officer who took my prints and mug shot. He was professional and kind. Not once did I feel condemned.

Also, the main jail supervisor showed great mercy. We had contact a few times throughout the night. In jail, I kept my head down and only answered when spoken to. Yet, throughout the process, the supervisor spoke to me with empathy. I felt as if somehow she knew the truth of what happened between my husband and me. Her compassion mystified me. Before returning me to the holding cell, she placed her hand on my shoulder, and sweetly said, "You are going to get through this." I never forgot her words. God would use several people that night to convey His love and concern for me through the use of words, telling me, "You are not alone."

God spoke to me through another inmate. While sitting in the holding cell, a small-framed young woman entered and spoke to me immediately. I looked up from the cement bench and noticed that she had cuts and scrapes on her knee and lip. We made eye contact. She said, "Girrrrrl, why you cryin, God's with you." Her words told me that God was with me.

The young woman sat down and sang old church hymns. Even slumped over, I listened. The rhythm of the song she sang was familiar though the words were new to me. At first, I felt comforted by her singing. Then, after a few moments, I felt tightness in my chest. A lump filled my throat while sadness overflowed the rest of me. As she sang about the Holiness of God, it hit me. I was a sinner! I put myself in that cell! God used the words of the praise hymn she sang to not only convict my heart, but He had proven the spoken word, mattered!

In jail, words brought me comfort and clarity. Ironically, words spoken by myself and my husband earlier the same night resulted in sin and pain. In one night, I would learn a powerful lesson about words that would bring about the most important change God would make in me. Through this experience, God would forever change what I said to others.

Unlike before this night, God would now compel me to think before I spoke. If I tried to speak without thinking first, I became tongue tied or completely forgot my train of thought. Sometimes, I would even forget a simple word when speaking. Other times, I could feel the wheels spinning in my head. It felt like those times when I was first learning to speak Spanish. I knew what I wanted to say, but simply couldn't translate the words in my head. Was God changing the words *I* wanted to say to what *He* wanted me to say? The only time, I didn't struggle to speak freely, was while praising God. Then and only then, God would allow my words to flow.

The change God made in my speech was a gift. Since, I no longer spoke my mind using thoughtless comments, I no longer spent an exorbitant amount of time cleaning up my mess and apologizing. This is not to say that I don't still struggle with words. I am still working on breaking the habit of interrupting and dominating conversations. Yet, throughout the past two years, God has enabled me to use words and impact others with His love.

I remember times when I hurt my children by teasing, judging and thoughtless comments. I wish I could go back and parent my children again. I know I would do certain things differently. For instance, instead of hurting my children with discouraging words, I would rely on help from the Holy Spirit and use words found in scripture to provide hope and comfort.

I especially regret one particular occasion with my niece. As my older sister's only child, my niece has had my heart in her hands since birth. Throughout her life, I have tried to play an influential role. Still today, she has a way of making me laugh until my sides hurt.

For weeks, I had been asking her to join the children's choir during one Christmas season at church. I led the children's choir and had already signed up several children. Still, I wanted my niece to join the choir too. Finally, one day, she came.

My sister had dressed my young niece beautifully. She wore her Sunday best and attempted to find a place next to another young girl in line. She was embarrassed and shy. Without hugging her or warmly welcoming her, I hurriedly handed her music sheets. She fumbled with the pages. I was impatient. It was as though I expected her to immediately possess the skill of reading music. Instead of showing her compassion and being overjoyed that she attended practice, I immediately made a sarcastic remark. In front of all of the other children and parents, I said, "Of course the one who is not ready yet, is my own family member." My niece looked humiliated. She simply hung her head.

When the practice was over, my sister grabbed my niece's hand and marched her out of the church without saying a word. My thoughtless remark had left an impression on my niece's heart. With one sentence, I diminished her hope, confidence and enthusiasm. I recall now, with great detail the backdrop of that moment. We were standing in the front of a church, next to a manger scene. The church was filled with Christian parents and children. We were there to glorify God through song. I was there to win souls. I had an opportunity to influence, support and encourage the spiritual life of others, especially my niece. Instead, I demonstrated the art of humiliation through sarcasm.

Nowadays, I think about all the children I could have led into a relationship with Jesus Christ. I could have told many children abandoned by their parents that God was with them and protecting them. I know now, I could have comforted my niece in the front of that church using the Word of God.

These days, I try to Glorify God in conversations with children. When I am open to guidance from the Holy Spirit, my words bring comfort and hope.

Recently, I witnessed to a foster child. My client participated in our church's annual Christmas play. She needed transportation to and from weekly practices and I volunteered to drive her.

While in the car one day, she told me about a slumber party she attended. This 12-year-old girl proudly announced she had stayed up until five o'clock in the morning. She told how a fight had occurred. I listened intently as she described the war raging through phone text messages. She and the other 12-year-old girls at the party were bored and texted a boy from school. This boy was not liked by the group of girls at the party. Consequently, the text messages were filled with anger. Within minutes the girls at the party told the boy how much he was disliked. The final text message contained pure hatred as the girls wrote the words, "Why don't you go kill yourself." The boy replied, "Maybe I will." I found it difficult to focus my attention on the road while also trying to process the story she told. My client continued on.

Worried that the boy was seriously considering hurting himself, my client called the boy's home and admitted to his mother how she and her friends had bullied the boy. Then we pulled up to the home for play practice. We sat for awhile in the car. It was my turn to respond. I told her words can have a profound effect on someone. I spoke about how God used the words of others to change my life. I talked about scripture and compassion.

As I spoke, I thought about the mighty words of John 3:16, "For God so loved the world that He gave His only begotten Son, that whoever believes in Him should not perish but have everlasting life." (NKJV). These words teach hope, love and forgiveness. It felt for a moment, as if *I* were learning these words for the first time. "How I could have ever thought that words didn't matter?"

I walked into the Christmas play practice with the marvelous feeling that I possibly led a child towards a deeper relationship with Christ. I will always remember the power of words, dear Lord, especially Your words.

I ask for forgiveness from all of the children, *especially my niece*, for my hurtful words throughout the years. I know now, I have a responsibility to communicate God's love through words. I am sorry for my past angry tones and mean words which I used out of my own selfishness. "If you are a child I hurt with my words, please forgive me!"

CHAPTER TEN

FROM UNANSWERED PRAYERS TO ANSWERED PRAYERS

Isaiah 1:15. When you spread out your hands, I will hide My eyes from you; Even though you make many prayers, I will not hear. Your hands are full of blood (NKJV).

When I indulged in sin yet prayed, God would not hear me. In fact, according to scripture, He refused to look. But when I repented, asked for forgiveness and prayed, God demonstrated that there was no limit to His reply.

While in my twenties, I prayed to God for help with a situation involving a landlord who decided to keep my security deposit. The landlord said she was keeping the money because I owned a cat without paying a pet deposit and that the cat had damaged the carpet. She was right. I lied about having a pet, didn't leave a deposit and my cat had urinated on the carpet several times in the same spot. Despite all of this, I prayed for God to fix the problem by returning my security deposit. I felt I was entitled to the money, after all I thought, "I kept the rest of the apartment in spotless condition." What I realize now, is that I was asking God to reward me for lying. I was asking God to do my will. No wonder He didn't respond.

A large part of the healing process of October 2008 was learning the purpose of prayer. Further, I had to learn *how* to pray. Prayer, as demonstrated in my home growing up, was a repetitious act. Speaking directly to the Father on the other hand, in my own words, through His Son was much more difficult. I didn't know what to say. My past behavior still had a grip on my heart. Therefore, in the beginning, it was difficult to have a contrite heart while praying. I began to pray before I prayed. I asked God for the right words to say and when I couldn't express my true feelings and anger was my only feeling, I would use His words and pray "The Lord's Prayer."

Today, my husband and I still laugh at his words when we first prayed together. We had been fighting and couldn't come to a resolution. One day, we were very frustrated and talking out our feelings just made it worse. I asked my husband to pray for us as a family and he said, "Okay." His prayer began, "Dear Lord, please help Donna." I began to laugh and corrected him saying, "*We* need help, not just me." I remember that, like my husband, many of *my* first prayers to God felt awkward. I paused to say "umm" frequently. At the end of one prayer, I remember saying, "Goodbye." It was only through the Holy Spirit that my prayers matured. He gave me words to speak. I noticed my prayers, with time, sounded less spiteful, had fewer pauses and I felt less embarrassment.

As holiness softly crept into my heart, I found myself crying as I prayed. And sometimes my soul responded and the words just flew from my mouth. I often found myself baffled at how my once judgmental, deceitful, cursing and divisive tongue had changed so dramatically. My prayers became more sacred and I witnessed an impact in others as I prayed for them and their loved ones. I also noticed that things really began to happen when I prayed. God began to hear my heart and respond!

One day, prompted by the Holy Spirit while in Wal-Mart, I purchased a cheap, little wipe-erase board and put it on the wall at home. I placed a picture of Jesus above the board. The first names I wrote on the board were of those who I perceived had hurt me. I was praying for my own healing. Soon my heart opened up towards them and I began to pray for their needs.

Within weeks, I started adding names to the board. These were people that I spoke to in the grocery store, bank and on the street. Each day, the board would catch my eye as I entered my bedroom. I found myself purposefully glancing at it and whichever name caught my eye, became my next prayer. I would then pray for the individual's specific need. I prayed for God to use the life of my new homeless friend, and help him to feel a purpose in living again. I prayed for family members in need of physical and/or emotional healing. I prayed for the husband of a grocery store clerk to gain employment. I prayed for peace for a woman going through a divorce. Consistently, I prayed for my personal family to reunite under one roof and to give God first priority in all our lives. Many times these prayers left me in tears and drained of energy.

Soon, I began to pray throughout the day. Whenever I looked at the prayer board, I stopped and took time to pray for someone. Even while studying in bed, and facing my prayer board, I'd pray, intermittently, for hours as I read assignments and prepared for tests.

The prayer board evolved into a miracle. It awakened my heart as I spoke my own words to God. And the more I used it, the greater my personal faith grew. I loved telling people that I had been praying for them because positive things would happen. Initially, I felt very uncomfortable and a little embarrassed to walk up to strangers and tell them that I was praying for them. But the usual and very grateful response was enough for me to joyfully press on. Days later, I would run into that person who would inevitably say, "You are never going to believe what happened!" The stories they told exceeded my hopefulness without fail! Time after time, their testimonies of God's answer to my prayers brought tears. I couldn't really fathom that God was hearing and responding to me! His answers to my prayers and, subsequently, the blessing I received upon hearing their heartfelt stories increased my faith significantly. To others, God began to exist in a very real way. To me, God had filled a void and sense of abandonment that I had felt for years.

A domino effect soon began. I shared with the next person I was now praying for a real story from the prayer board. As I shared, the person said to me, "I just got goose bumps." I began to understand that I was not working alone. God was allowing the Holy Spirit to work within me to reach others. Those goose bumps were a confirmation that the Holy Spirit truly touches hearts in the exact moment that I testify about God and what He can and will do.

Soon God was laying a burden of purpose on my heart. I began to feel compassion for those who had deeply hurt me. I didn't question when God would next prompt me to specifically help them: I simply obeyed. I purchased gifts, left nice notes edifying them, spoke highly of them during conversations with others and prayed for them in private. At one point, I found myself acting with loving kindness towards those who were still persecuting me. Eventually, I noticed these people seemed to struggle with their anger towards me and my anger from past pain was vanishing.

I heard a song recently that described my experience of surrendering my pain to God through prayer. The song called, "What a friend we have in Jesus" was written by Joseph M. Scriven over a century ago.

What A Friend [We Have in Jesus]
Text: Joseph M. Scriven, 1820-1886
Music: Charles C. Converse, 1832-1918

What a friend we have in Jesus,
All our sins and grief to bear!
What a privilege to carry
everything to God in prayer!
Oh, what peace we often forfeit,
Oh, what needless pain we bear,
all because we do not carry
everything to God in prayer!
Have we trials and temptations?
Is there trouble anywhere?
We should never be discouraged—
Take it to the Lord in prayer.
Can we find a friend so faithful,
Who will all our sorrows, share?
Jesus knows our every weakness;
Take it to the Lord in prayer.

How true these words are! Over the past two years, I have carried all my burdens to Jesus through prayer. In doing so, Jesus has brought me a sense of peace and an understanding that I am not alone in my pain. I know now, that I may experience hurtful moments in my life by others who offend or persecute me. I also know to carry pain to God in prayer and that he will exchange it for a feeling of peace. Prayer continues to be a miraculous breakthrough in my life.

My prayer board.

CHAPTER ELEVEN

FROM TROUBLE MAKER TO COMFORTER

Proverbs 11:29 He who troubles his own house will inherit the wind, and the fool will be servant to the wise of heart (NKJV).

Coming from an upbringing that was more chaotic than peaceful, it became more comfortable to stir things up and live in chaos than in peace. Therefore, I often used my temper, anxiety and bitterness to disrupt peaceful situations. As Proverbs 11:29 suggests, by doing so, my actions never allowed me to hold onto anything that mattered. Instead, I inherited only the wind.

I suffered the effects of my behavior both professionally and personally. I never spent very long with one employer because of my habit of instigating problems, usually through gossip or power struggles. When the tension would rise at work, I'd quit. As a result, I became a job hopper.

I had the same habits in my personal relationships. I would deliberately cause a break-up with my boyfriend, and then begged for him to forgive and take me back. It was uncomfortable to be content. I didn't understand the meaning of peace and craved conflict and stress.

In my late 20's, I grew weary of the revolving door I had created. I made the decision to search for a solution. Friends and family were finding answers to similar problems through degrees of higher education. Therefore, I returned to school. I attended a graduate school and studied psychology. I even completed 80 hours of training to become certified as a domestic violence counselor. However, education from the field of psychology only taught me how to define behaviors. It provided no solution to my personal problems. For years to come, I lived my life from a worldly perspective and continued to seek worldly answers to my relationship problems.

After I moved into the apartment in 2008, I began to think about going back to school. For years, I had been focusing on maintaining my new family and didn't have much time for myself. In the apartment, I cared for my little son, yet needed something to occupy my mind at night. I considered obtaining a Ph.D. in psychology. But, God orchestrated several circumstances to change my mind. First, the Ph.D. program at my alma mater had increased in cost by

$10,000 and the school was not considered eligible for student loans. The thought of obtaining a Ph.D. from an eligible university entered my mind.

One day, I Googled "Ph.D. programs" on the computer and the school, Liberty University appeared on my screen. I called the school for more information. The enrollment counselor's approach was surprisingly respectful. I waited for him to aggressively promote the school or pressure me to enroll, but he remained calm and gracious. He even asked to pray with me over the decision to return to school. After one call, I knew in my heart, I was supposed to enroll at Liberty University.

I learned that my Master of Arts degree in psychology was not acceptable because it was obtained from a non-accredited university. I would have to obtain a Master's degree from an accredited university before enrolling in the Ph.D. program at Liberty University. I questioned, "What am I going to do with a second Master's degree?" At the same time, I was very excited at the thought of returning to school. I told myself, "I will apply for financial aid and if I am accepted, I will enroll."

I applied for one semester of financial aid to cover the first semester costs. I thought I could afford to pay out of pocket for the rest of the degree. When I received a check from Federal Student Aid, the amount covered the entire cost of the Master's Degree, almost to the dollar. I knew then, I was supposed to attend and graduate.

God continued to steer me to do His will. Each time I spoke with Liberty University staff, I felt a strange sense of being in the right place. I considered the available programs of study. I found myself captivated by several class titles under the Seminary Program. God had guided me in choosing the program and major for me. Then, to confirm His will, I learned I was eligible to receive a discount for my husband's military service. Within two weeks time, I was accepted into Theological Seminary and contemplated my first semester schedule.

The new semester began hurriedly. To complete each homework assignment, I needed to learn a new online system called Blackboard. It was very stressful. Then, on the first day of class, my only computer died. With a borrowed computer, I searched online and found a refurbished computer at a very reasonable price. I drove to Wal-Mart to purchase a cheap computer desk. I put the desk together myself. Now I had my writing area.

During the first week of school, I read Scripture. For the first time, I learned biblical History. I had so much to learn! I felt like I was traveling back in time and was fascinated with stories I read. Each narrative demonstrated characteristics of God. I read about God and His plan for me. The more I read, the more I became hungry for the Word.

Since I didn't know if there was a right way to read scripture, I just let it speak for itself. Each day, I'd let my bible fall open to whatever page and begin reading with the first bold chapter number on the page. I read a chapter a day.

Beginning my day by reading the bible became an enjoyable new habit for me and set the tone for the entire day. In the past, I usually began my day with a hurried cup of coffee and quick check of my banking records and email, before rushing on to the next task. Now, reading the bible came first before anything else. It was easy to put God first because I craved Him.

God would meet daily with me to share a private moment. His word provided perfect encouragement and discipline. I started to cherish those early morning moments. I sat in my living room chair facing a window. Sometimes, the sun would peer through the window. On one instance, after whispering, "Good morning God," a beam of sun light shined directly on me and my bible below. Each day, God spoke to my heart with the exact words I needed to hear. There were even times I woke with a thought or question in my mind and immediately received a response through scripture.

Reading my bible surrounded me with a sense of serenity that I had never known before. The more I persisted, the more calm I became. I found comfort in God's word. I especially found reassurance in scripture when I felt attacked by others.

As I became calmer, I noticed my peers at work and my supervisor were not prepared for me to undergo transformation and suddenly act righteously. The attacks came. However, for the first time, I was not waging war or retaliating. Instead, I read my bible for answers. As I prayed for my adversaries, scripture prepared me for the attacks. I noticed the more I tried to walk with Jesus, the more they would attack. The more I would pray. When I didn't engage in the battle, I was excluded and rejected from social gatherings at work. I was being set apart from anyone who acted like the "old me." One quiet morning, through God's word, I learned that we are called to be set apart.

He then used the words of my university class-mates to comfort me with counsel regarding dis-tancing and rejection. God also used Scripture to teach me to run to Him during trials. As others attacked, I felt safe in the arms of God. By relying on Him, I was learning to leave feelings of stress and anxiety behind.

God also used circumstances to teach me peace and trust. Another consequence of my arrest was to face a tense and career threatening situation. As a Social Worker, being fingerprinted caused a red flag with the Department of Social Services. I received a call from an agent with the Department of Social Services months after the criminal charges were dropped. The Licensing Agent's demeanor was humiliating. She told me, "I know what you did. I have the papers right in front of me. You need to fax court documents to our office immediately!" I tried to explain that I was the victim, but she didn't want to listen. I faced great uncertainty regarding my career which I had excelled in for over two decades. Rather than fight back, I prayed and read scripture. God reassured me. He had me read 2 Corinthians 1:4, which says, "God comforted me so that I could comfort others in their time of trouble (NKJV)." His supportive presence chased away my fear.

I faxed the paperwork, and in a second conver-sation with the agent, I was finally able to explain what had really happened. I thought I heard her cry on the other side of the phone before we ended the call. I received a letter from the Department of Social Services about two weeks later stating that I was fit to provide care to children.

Learning about God has caused me to reflect on my past behavior. I ran from deep, personal relationships because I hadn't learned to be a child of God. I felt depressed and blamed my sadness on others when I was just feeling lost without God and shameful for my sins. The day I accepted the gift of His sacrifice on the cross was the day that I experienced God's love for me. His love has calmed my soul. I finally live peacefully.

Today, when I see a person suffering from emotional pain and hear his heartbreaking story, I am reminded of my own journey. I am reminded of scripture. I imagine the person as a lost sheep. I feel a need in me to tell him, "Life does not have to be so painful. The Good Shepherd wants all of His sheep to come home. He loves you and misses you. God is waiting for you to come to Him with your pain!"

I wish *I* had made the choice for God years ago. I am so thankful I ran to God and repented! I ask myself each day, "Where would I be without You Lord?"

John 10:14-15

I am the good shepherd; and I know My *sheep,* and am known by My own. As the Father knows Me, even so I know the Father; and I lay down My life for the sheep. (NKJV)

CHAPTER TWELVE

FROM CONTROLLING TO TRUSTING IN GOD

Proverbs 3:5 Trust in the Lord with all your heart, And lean not on your own understanding; In all your ways acknowledge Him, And He shall direct your paths (NKJV).

L earning to open my heart to God's will was the hardest lesson I had to learn. It meant I had to let go of all of my anxieties, plans and fears and lean on His understanding and plans for me. What a blessing true surrender would bring!

From an early age, I had made plans for how my life would turn out. I dreamed of owning an orphanage, singing a Disney "hit" love song and beginning a family. On paper, I had my life mapped out to the year. I planned on being married by age 25, having children and a doctorate degree by age thirty and owning my first home at 35. I tried to meet these goals on my own but was unprepared for the detours my life would take along the way.

I knew for many years my life didn't work, no matter how much I tried to manipulate and control it. Ironically, the more that I felt out of control inside, the more I tried to control my life and others around me. I had to learn what it meant to surrender to God's will before I could learn how to finally live in peace. Once I surrendered my life to God's will, I began to cherish my life.

Just like surrendering negative aspects of my personality, letting go of ultimate control took great effort, and was not easily accomplished. God was merciful though. He used scripture and songs to confirm His presence and blessed me with comfort each time I chose to let go.

The night I experienced the greatest loss of control was the night I found myself sitting in the patrol car with handcuffs digging into my wrists. God had to capture my attention by cuffing my hands and by taking my son, my home and my belongings away. As those handcuffs came off my wrists, I began surrendering my life to God. At that moment, I didn't know how I was going to live my life without trying to control everyone and everything around me. All I knew was what I was doing was not working. Without delay, Jesus confirmed His presence to me in the holding cell. He saved me and I immediately, I found shelter in Him. He became my only hope, so for the first time in my life, I surrendered control to Jesus.

Because I felt such strength and encouragement in surrendering to Jesus that night, I started to turn to Jesus when I felt my life was going out of my control. I remember the week that my youngest son and I moved into our apartment. Suddenly, my son started hitting me. I was so shocked. He had no prior history of hitting and had not witnessed the violence in October 2008 between his father and me. However, now my son's anger for my choice to separate us from his father was directed onto me. From my four-year-old son's perspective, I was holding him back from his daddy and he was furious with me.

Over the next month or two, there were many days and nights I would have to watch my child dissolve. I knew that I needed to be strong for him, but there were times that I didn't have the energy. I had to hire the movers, deal with my enraged husband and schedule services such as gas and electric in the apartment. At the same time, I was still working over forty hours a week as a Social Worker, and trying to manage fifteen foster children who had their own critical issues. I felt consumed at work and overwhelmed with responsibility in my personal life.

One night, I sat at my computer desk to create a "to do" list. My eyes welled with tears as I thought about the responsibilities I faced. Weary, I placed the pencil on the desk and cried out loud to the Lord for help. Just then, the internet site that streamed music into my computer, played a song. My heart melted when the artist began to sing. Through the song, God confirmed I needed to let go and let Him have His way. I threw up my hands and hung my head as I continued to weep.

I was amazed that it didn't feel crazy about my hands up in the air, since I had never worshiped this way before. While the same song played suggesting that I let go and let God, I kneeled down to pray. I felt an unfamiliar urge to place my forehead on the floor and stretch my hands out as if I was reaching to touch the Lord's feet. In this position, I sobbed. I thought, "I need you God. Help me please. I can't do this without you!" Right away, the artist sang, "You don't have to cry, 'cause I'll supply all your needs." I continued to weep. I felt like I cried every last tear before rising from the floor.

The next day, my son began to tell me, "Mommy, I love you. You're a pretty girl. You're my best friend, my whole life." Through those words, God confirmed He had my life under control and all I had to do was turn to Him for direction and help. I was finally able to loosen my grip and let go.

Over the next week, God continued to reveal how He had been waiting patiently to help me with my life and in raising my son. He encouraged and strengthened me through wise counsel from others. For example, during a visit with my son's childhood physician, the doctor revealed that he was a Christian.

This certain doctor had been treating my son for over four years and we had never spoken about God. On this visit however, when I asked him for advice regarding my son's picky eating, he answered with a question. He asked "How long can man go without eating or drinking?" I remained quiet when he then responded, "Well, we know that man can live up to forty days without food and water, and your four-year-old will not even come close to that time without eating." I smiled and said, "You're a Christian." He smiled and nodded as if he had been waiting for the right moment to tell me.

As a result of letting go, I noticed several changes in me. First, my eyes were opened to see God in every detail of my life. I started to believe there are no accidents, no coincidences, it's not Karma, nor is it "What goes around comes around." I don't have hunches, intuition or another sense. It's all God's doing!

Also, I have noticed His ability to be extremely detail oriented. Many times, I couldn't explain what was happening or why. I excitedly stated, "It must be a God thing." I understood for the first time God had a plan and a will for me. It was overwhelming to see how God used one situation to affect so many people. And it was incredibly freeing for me not to consistently worry about the details.

Next, my attitude transformed from overbearing to trusting and peaceful. I remember the first time I noticed this change.

One night my parents came to visit. We ordered a large meat lovers pizza from a local pizza restaurant. Our order took extra time to arrive at our home and when we opened the box, it was a combination pizza instead of the meat lovers we had ordered. My mother asked if I was going to call the restaurant to complain. She said that I should at least get my money back. I simply stated, "I trust God. Maybe if we had eaten the meat lovers, we would have gotten sick. It's possible that the meat was bad. *This* is the pizza that God wants for us. We should give thanks for what He has given us. And it is not for us to understand His ways." My family looked at me in amazement!

The old Donna would have stopped at nothing to have an employee embarrassed and humiliated for making a simple mistake. In this instance, I was calm and gracious.

Then, I began to wrestle with my career choice. After decades of social work, I started to struggle with the title "Social Worker." I realized my work role was to label others according to their behavior, such as drug addict. In order to accomplish my job, I had to judge others for their actions. Then I was required to document each person's negative behavior and this became a permanent record for others to read. It was then my job to provide evidence that each person was progressively becoming a more "successful" individual in society. And success was determined according to specific worldly definitions. As a condition of my employment, I was forbidden to tell others about God's grace and forgiveness.

As I recognized my own shortcomings and sinful past, I began to resist my job duties. Through Scripture, I learned that Jesus Christ is the only judge of each man. Therefore, I no longer felt worthy to judge others.

While this knowledge compelled me to look for another profession, I also found it liberating. I began to see people differently. I no longer saw individuals as my problem to solve. In fact, I found myself identifying more with all people since we are all sinners. I was especially drawn to those who had been humbled by their own behavior. In fact, I preferred being around the humble and meek rather than the self-righteous. I knew I was changing inside.

Consequently, my perception of negative behavior changed. I began to see destructive behavior as a symptom of pain and separation from God. I finally understood the solution! I couldn't keep quiet about this good news. I started to explain my new belief to clients. I said, "The further we go from God, the more pain we experience. To escape from pain, we turn to drugs and other destructive behaviors. But God loves us all and is waiting for us to return to His loving arms. All we have to do is say we are sorry and He will forgive us and welcome us home. Jesus can take away our pain."

I have learned over the past two years, that surrendering every detail to God, without understanding the why, and how, leads to freedom. I keenly remember the result of trying to "help" others in the past and how I relied on my own understanding and needs at the time. I remember feeling resentful when the person did not react as I expected. Now that I trust in the Lord with all my heart, I no longer feel resentment, anxiety or a need to control.

God's blessings come when I rely on my Father in Heaven for guidance!

CHAPTER THIRTEEN

FROM GOSSIP TO FAITHFUL SPIRIT

Proverbs 11:13 The talebearer reveals secrets, But he who is of a faithful spirit conceals matter (NKJV).

As a gossip, I revealed secrets and was not a trustworthy listener. However, since growing in faith, I have become more deserving of confidence. Nowadays, the only secrets I make public, are my own.

I loved to gossip. I couldn't resist sharing my opinion and judging others for their behavior. I used gossiping to build relationships with others and get attention. Mostly, I gossiped out of revenge. If I was hurt by something someone did and felt powerless to speak directly to the person about it, I spoke behind their back. Other times, gossiping made me feel superior. I spent many hours trying to rally people to take my side of an argument, and quite frankly, I felt that I was convincing. I read once that gossip is anything that you say which causes another person to think negatively about someone else. I realize now I behaved in a manner contrary to what Jesus taught. I was to walk in love and edify others with my words. Instead I used words as a divisive tool and to tear others down.

When I fully realized what I was doing was not pleasing to God, I began to start down the road of stopping myself. I committed to no longer participating in gossip. I refused to listen to gossip from others. Through scripture, I was learning another way to handle being hurt. Forgiveness!

Because I never knew how to offer forgiveness to others, I had to learn. The experience with my husband was a perfect opportunity to teach me. It caused me to examine my choices. I could forgive him, save my marriage, and offer him the grace that God gave me through His Son's death, or I could divorce him, hold on to the pain and become even angrier and more resentful. Unlike in the past, this time, I chose to follow Jesus' example and offer forgiveness. For awhile, I struggled daily with not gossiping to others about my perception of the night in October 2008. I felt entitled to compassion and sympathy. I had to pray daily for God to help me forgive my husband. At the time, I had no idea how forgiveness would later bless me and my children as well as my husband. I believe it was choosing to forgive that eventually led my husband to go to church and begin a relationship with Christ.

A nun once taught me her understanding of the concept of forgiveness. She said, "If you can remember what it was that you were supposed to forgive, you haven't forgiven the person yet." Perhaps this is partially true. Through my recent experience with my husband, I have learned that even after you have let go of a hurt and forgiven the person, the memory remains, but the pain goes away. In my case, when I talk about the night of October 2008 today, it's as if I am describing something which happened to someone else. I remember the event in detail, but I am not ashamed, hurt or angry anymore. To my surprise, I am grateful for the lessons God taught me through the experience.

The bible helps me to remember that I am a sinner who just two years ago loved to put others down in conversation. I also try to pray for understanding as to what someone else may be going through. This keeps me humble and continually softens my heart towards others who hurt me. And I pray for grace. For me, forgiveness is not just a one prayer occurrence, but a process. It takes time to let God graciously heal the heart. I have been blessed in learning to forgive. God has shown me great mercy and has healed my heart as He promised.

CHAPTER FOURTEEN

FROM PRIDE AND SHAME TO HUMILITY AND SUBMISSION TO CHRIST

Proverbs 11:2 When pride comes, then comes shame; But with the humble is wisdom (NKJV).

As a proud person, I deceived myself. I often ignored when others suggested a reality different than mine. My arrogance habitually pressured me to conduct myself in a way, deep down, I knew wasn't right. I would often find myself later, feeling ashamed of the way I had spoken to others. I frequently found myself later apologizing. In contrast, after I became humble, God filled me with His wisdom and the Holy Spirit. I saw who I was before and how I exalted myself. I was finally able to recognize God's role in my life and walk as His humble servant.

If you ask someone who knew me before October 2008, you might hear the opinion "She thought highly of herself." Almost everything I said spoke to how self-absorbed I was. I had a habit of verbally providing my resume in every conversation. I relied on my educational background to impress others. I even had a few usual comments that would automatically roll off my tongue when I didn't get my way or when I thought I had accomplished something great. When others didn't meet my expectations, I would say, "Who do I need to talk to?" I believed I was a strong woman who shouldn't have to take "no" for an answer.

This was especially true, when I felt slighted or overcharged for an item in a store. I stopped at nothing to have a person reprimanded if I didn't receive the humble apology I felt I deserved.

One of the worst instances of my ego occurred one day while my husband and I were still living on the naval installation. For weeks, the gardeners' foul language echoed through our bathroom window. On this day, I had become fed up with listening to their cursing at each other. So, I decided to confront the group of men. Aggravated, I marched out to the lawn and began to yell, "Hey, you need to watch your mouths, there are children around here!" Almost instantly, a man from across the street came to intercede. As he walked up to my door, he asked, "Are you Donna?" I said, "Yes." Then the man politely introduced himself. He smiled when he told me his name. I shook my head as I realized he was a past childhood friend. We hadn't seen each other in years. He told me that the men in the group were his clients and that I should have a little patience. I was so embarrassed! In my arrogance, I had yelled at a group of men who were developmentally delayed for using profanity in their lunch conversation.

But God had a plan in helping me conquer my pride. The plan included two phases. The first phase began the night I called the police on October 20, 2008, to teach my husband a lesson. In my arrogance, I thought I was calling the police to win the fight. I wanted my husband to understand that "No one who lays a hand on me can get away with it." That night, I learned God was in charge.

As I waited to meet with the bail bondsman, I sat with my head bowed and my shoulders slumped. I felt vulnerable and helpless. For the first time in years, I allowed my sense of meekness to surface. At first, it was hard to feel anything but the familiar anger and defensiveness I had become so accustomed to. I felt myself wanting to focus on the issues of the other detainees. But in my own brokenness, just after everything I once held dear had been taken from me, I felt speechless and unqualified.

So I decided to feel the emotions that begged to surface. As a result, I felt my life's deepest moment of despair. The feeling of pain was so engrossing, I began to wonder if God still loved me. For a moment, I felt like I was seven-years-old again standing at the window, crying for my father to come home. I cried out to God for help! He immediately responded to my cry and walked into the cell. He was in every word of the strangers I met. He was in the song of a cell mate and later the same night, He wrapped His arms around me through a friend, my mother and stepfather.

After that night, my perspective on life changed. I began to see my arrest as a wake up call from God. I wondered if God had stopped me down my road to Damascus. When I realized how far I had ran from the presence of God and how much I still needed Him, I decided to leave pride and arrogance far behind.

I felt sadness for sinning against God. I began to repent daily and admitted my faults and shortcomings to family and friends. For hours on end, I vocally confessed my sins. As a result, my heart began to change. I regained sensitivity to others again and felt an instant sorrow and regret when I acted ugly. I took my wickedness straight to God and would quickly apologize to His Son, Jesus Christ when I perceived that my words and actions hurt others.

In return, God never left my side. I felt a complete sense of relief. The familiar feelings of pain, confusion and disorder were quickly disappearing and I felt new. I cried a lot. Sometimes I cried from a repentant heart and sometimes from feelings of delight.

At first, the feeling of joy was very uncomfortable. I felt like others might think I had gone crazy. But I was feeling a sense of relief and I wanted to tell everyone about my experience. I felt an inner sense of completeness erase many years of feeling broken. I no longer felt lost and lonely. Instead, I felt like I was coming home to a peaceful and loving welcome.

Around this time, God led me to read Hebrews chapter twelve.

[5] And you have forgotten the exhortation which speaks to you as to sons: "My son, do not despise the chastening of the LORD, Nor be discouraged when you are rebuked by Him; [6] For whom the LORD loves He chastens, And scourges every son whom He receives. [7] If you endure chastening, God deals with you as with sons; for what son is there whom a father does not chasten? [8] But if you are without chastening, of which all have become partakers, then you are illegitimate and not sons. [9] Furthermore, we have had human fathers who corrected us, and we paid them respect. Shall we not much more readily be in subjection to the Father of spirits and live? [10] For they indeed for a few days chastened us as seemed best to them, but He for our profit, that we may be partakers of His holiness. [11] Now no chastening seems to be joyful for the present, but painful; nevertheless, afterward it yields the peaceable fruit of righteousness to those who have been trained by it." Hebrews 12:5-11 (New King James Version).

Through Hebrews, God made it clear to me to accept His correction because it was done from love. For the first time, I began to comprehend God's heart. I realized how holy God is. My view of God began to change as I thought, "Maybe God wanted me to be holy too. Maybe I was shaken from life in this way so that I would develop such a distaste to sin that I didn't want to sin anymore. I am sure God knew the shame I felt from being prideful. Maybe God wanted to prevent me from feeling ashamed in the future." Those first weeks began my journey to becoming humble. The second phase of God's plan included employing the lives of those around me to teach me humility.

About a year after my arrest, I was studying one night and heard a loud noise upstairs. The man who lived upstairs was very pleasant and we exchanged greetings each day. He was very kind to my young son and often watched him kick the ball in the front yard area. I didn't respond to the noise upstairs that night, because I had grown used to noises heard through the thin walls of the apartment. The next day, I was completely shocked to learn that my upstairs neighbor committed suicide. I mourned that I hadn't spoken to this neighbor about hope through Christ. I was a Seminarian and was too afraid of feeling rejected to bring up Jesus Christ in conversations with others. I blamed myself for not being an instrument of hope to this man.

Around the same time, a homeless woman in our town was suddenly hit and killed by a car while crossing the freeway one night. My youngest son and I had become close to her. Again, I mourned for how little I spoke about God to this woman prior to her death. I promised myself to bring up God in every future conversation.

God continued the theme of loss to humble me. Our family dog contracted cancer. She had surgery, but the cancer returned aggressively. We had to put her to sleep. Then my supervisor suddenly cut my work hours in half. I had to receive unemployment for the first time to afford a living for my son and myself.

Through each of these humbling experiences, I felt sorrow and a sense of helplessness, and I turned to God. In return, I felt the warming presence of the Holy Spirit. With my decision to put my pride aside, He comforted me. Unlike the past, during times of loss, on these occasions, I never felt alone.

I prayed for the Holy Spirit to use each heart-breaking situation to glorify God through me. He did. The Holy Spirit led me to help someone who survived the loss of my upstairs' neighbor. We later became close friends. He guided me to the boyfriend of the homeless woman. I was able to pray with him through *his* loss. And He helped me understand why it was important for me to work part-time. It was an incredible opportunity to enroll full-time in school and learn more about God.

My transformation to a more humble person had a surprising effect. I even watched those around me begin to lose their arrogance and self-pride. Just shortly after I moved out of our home, I found myself needing extra money to afford dental surgery. To pay for the surgery, I sold our family dining room table. In response, my husband impulsively purchased another table for our family home.

Over two years passed and my husband had not used the new dining room table. When he moved to Florida for work, he asked me to help him sell the table. So I placed an ad on a local internet site.

I immediately received a call. The woman, who responded to the ad, told me she was a Christian. She talked about her desire to help a new member of her church. I felt touched as the woman spoke about the new church member's story. I learned that the new member was a young woman with two children who was forced to leave her home to escape abuse. I shared my story with the woman too. There was no doubt in my mind; my husband was to donate the table to the new church member. I called him at work to explain the situation. He enthusiastically supported my desire to donate the table. As God would have it, my husband's purchase ironically provided support to an abused female.

Through God and God alone, I was able to conquer pride and become humble. I began to see trials as a precious time to praise God and witness to His favor. I have since replaced my old favorite saying with a new one. Instead of saying, "Who do I need to talk to" and insisting on getting my way or pointing out another's mistakes, I frequently say, "There is only one God, and His name is not Donna."

CHAPTER FIFTEEN

FROM BIG SPENDER TO INSTRUMENT FOR GOD

**Proverbs 11:28 He who trusts in
his riches will fall,
But the righteous will flourish
like foliage (NKJV).**

Greed and selfishness caused me to make sinful choices regarding money. Money management was one of my greatest failures. Yet, once I fully committed my heart to God, He revealed the true meaning of prosperity and forever changed how I viewed money.

During the first few weeks in college, I frequented the bookstore and other places on campus often. Each time I passed by the front of the bookstore at my new college, my eyes were drawn to a certain table. It had a nice tablecloth and two bank representatives smiling behind it. A bank was offering a line of credit to students. I was lured to the table one day by one of the representatives who asked me if I "wanted to build my credit." What a trap! It was my first time living away from my parents and I was trying to make it on my own. In fact, the day I left for college, I fought with my parents and swore my independence.

I quickly realized how fast bills add up, and I began to feel financially insecure. As I spoke with the representative that day, I felt a false sense of security. She emphasized the capability of withdrawing cash for emergencies. I completed the application unaware that I was on my way to material emptiness and credit card debt for the next ten years.

One credit card led to another and each came with a higher credit limit. I used the cards initially to defray the cost of rent, books and tuition, but it didn't take long before I was charging entertainment and nice furniture to my credit cards. I was living a lifestyle far beyond what God wanted for me. My cards seemed to impress others and became a great tool in distracting them from my ugly side. As long as I was spending money on people, I had friends.

I wish the bank representative at the table would have warned me that I would receive threatening calls until all hours of the night, feel an endless flood of guilt and shame and would lay awake for hours worrying about how I was going to pay off my debt. Why didn't she tell me that I would avoid contact and lie to collection agencies? If only I had trusted God to supply all my needs back then! I regret trying to live outside the means He provided for me.

In college, I didn't see who the employees behind the table actually represented and how my signature that day would lead me away from worshipping God. Consequently, I abused money for years before learning my lesson. While my credit is clear now, it is my surrender to God to take care of my family financially that brings me peace.

As with all other areas of my life, God taught me how to rely on Him financially. Again, He used situations and people to help me grow. Before I started the Master's degree program at Liberty, I examined my finances. Paying rent and all of the household bills was a new adjustment. It was obvious that I needed to apply for a loan for the first semester of school, but thereafter, I wanted to pay for school with my salary. I requested $1,500.00 in loans from the federal student aid program, known as FASFA. However, when the application was reviewed and the loan granted, I was offered $18,000.00. I immediately called the school to cancel the entire loan, but when I spoke with the student accounts department, the representative suggested that I pray about this decision. She informed me that once I paid off or denied any aid, I would have a difficult time requesting future loans. I did pray about returning most of the loan yet felt an overwhelming sense to leave the money in my student account for future use. Then my initial financial plan backfired. Suddenly, and without reason, my hours were cut in half at work. I knew then, what

God had already known. I would need all $18,000 to complete my degree.

God continued to teach me to trust Him with money. The first opportunity came while sitting in church one day. I had an overwhelming desire to write a check for a couple who were active church members. I didn't have the money in my checking account to cover the check and worried that I would be charged a $29.00 bank fee if the check was returned. But the feeling was overpowering. I heard myself say, "Okay Lord," out loud, and wrote the check. The amount I wrote the check for was $100.00. As I handed the check to the husband, he looked at me with surprise. I explained that I didn't understand why he was to receive this check, but God was clear that I was to give it to him. The man thanked me and we all left the church. Even though there is no mail service on Sunday, I had the same urgent feeling to check the mail. So, I went to the mailbox and opened it. Sure enough, I had mail. I must have forgotten to pick it up the day before. In the pile of mail was a check to me for $107.00. I began to cry. Once inside my apartment, I praised God and hit my knees. He was guiding *me* to help others. I was deeply affected that He trusted me with money. I heard at church the following week that the couple, due to the current bad economy, was experiencing hardship. I cried yet again and praised God.

These "money miracles" continued for two years. Each time, I would take a leap of faith and donate, write someone a check or give cash away (that I didn't have in my bank account), God immediately delivered the money to me. I found money in random places and received returned paid bills marked, "credit, do not pay." I also received a large tax refund when I had owed at tax time for years. Every time I was obedient in sharing money, it would come back and almost exactly to the penny. I started telling others my new nickname was "Even Steven."

My favorite money story involves my stepson and an opportunity for him to feel God's presence. My husband and stepson were moving out of our old home to consolidate belongings. Since my husband was now traveling with his company and my stepson was old enough to live on his own, my husband gave notice to the landlord of our larger rental home. My younger son and I were going to remain in our apartment, our new home. My husband commuted home on the weekends or as much as possible with his job.

My husband and my stepson needed to hire a cleaning crew to prepare the rental home for the new renters. My stepson came to me for assistance in hiring a cleaning company. I searched in the phone book and said a little prayer. Then I opened the phone book and it fell to a page that featured an ad that read, "God blessed my home, let me bless yours." By now, I felt comfortable with God speaking to me, so I had to chuckle. I called the owner of the business and explained the situation. She was happy to help us.

When I told her that my stepson was paying for the cleaning cost and that his finances were limited, she agreed to clean the 2,000 square foot home for $80.00. I called my stepson to inform him of the day, time and cost for her to clean. For a moment, the call went silent. My stepson then said he had spent the money in his savings account and had already asked his father, my husband, for a loan to pay for the cleaning. The amount my husband transferred into my stepson's account was exactly $80.00. This was the day that my stepson began to see the power of prayer and the presence of God in his life.

I have since developed a completely different relationship with money. Greed and selfishness are gone. I no longer feel that money is "mine." Instead, I believe money is a way of accomplishing God's will. In opening my heart to God and developing a deeper relationship with Him, He has given me a steady stream of financial blessings. I sleep in peace at night knowing that God supplies all my needs. I pray that He will continue to use me as an instrument for financially blessing others.

CHAPTER SIXTEEN

FROM EXAGGERATING AND LYING TO GOD'S TRUTH

Proverbs 11:1 Dishonest scales are an abomination to the Lord, But a just weight is His delight (NKJV).

God tells us through Proverbs11:1, He hates liars but delights in those who are honest. Recently, I learned why.

Prior to October 2008, I told lies, countless lies. The habit started at an early age. As a young child, I omitted some of the truth, embellished facts and exaggerated. This led me to get attention. As an adult, the habit continued. On October 20, 2008, a lie profoundly affected my life. Consequently, I have told the truth ever since.

I grew up in a home where the story of my life was very different from my peers. By age five, I had experienced a traumatic fire, several moves to different homes and my biological father leaving and returning to our home. When I spoke about these trials with schoolmates, they would walk away and say, "Come on, let's go play over here." As a result, I felt embarrassed, rejected and very alone.

By second grade, the truth seemed unbelievable. About this time, my sister and I saw our father fall from the roof onto the cement in our backyard. My mother was at work and my sister and I were alone to respond to my father's accident. I couldn't talk about what happened because the pain and the trauma were something that my friends couldn't relate to. *Their* home life appeared peaceful. I knew also, that my father had been in jail. As far as I knew, none of my friends' parents had even committed crimes. However, my friends were curious and began asking questions about my family. "Where is your father?" asked my friends. Since my mother did not explain what was happening within our family, I had no answers. I learned to create stories.

Looking back, it seemed like very little time had passed before my mother met my stepfather and remarried. My stepfather attended all of my school events and functions and was always at home. However, his presence only added to my confusion. I didn't know how to address this new man. Later, my biological father disappeared from the picture, and we had no contact. I didn't realize my stepfather was actually replacing my biological father, so I addressed him by the nickname everyone else used. My friends were as confused as I was to the structure of my old and new family. It was awkward to speak the truth when I didn't even know the truth.

Unlike my friends, whose biological parents were still married and living in the same home, my life included a mother and stepfather. At school and birthday functions, I saw their mothers and fathers together and I was envious. To counteract my feelings of envy, I began to lie. By then, I was lying for several reasons. I lied to cover up the behavior of my parents, to avoid embarrassment, to fit in and because I didn't understand what was real and truthful.

However, the number one reason I lied was for attention. I quickly discovered to interject humor and make others laugh. In my adult years, I found that I could walk into any room and convince others to stop and listen to my incredible stories. I could easily have center stage if I told stories with animated characters.

I knew as a child, to lie was a sin, but I could not understand "why" when it brought me instant relief from pain and embarrassment. When I lied, I fit in! When I told the truth, I felt alone.

I realized the night in October 2008 when my husband lied and I lost everything why God detests this sinful behavior. Suddenly, I clearly saw the consequences of a lie. Lying brings pain and suffering! I started to see that those childhood friends I made through lies, never remained friends and the attention I received was only temporary. What remained was a constant feeling of guilt and shame. I spent much of my life worried I would get caught in a lie.

After the night of October 20, 2008, I vowed to never lie again. God helped me keep my vow. He made me increasingly sensitive to lies and half-truths. When I started to lie or heard a lie told in my presence, I felt nauseous.

Telling the truth felt more natural as time progressed. God instructed me all the way. He used several measures to reach me. One of the ways He caught my attention was through a small, yellow book.

While waiting for a prescription for my youngest son's allergies at a supermarket, my eyes focused on a book by the medication counter. I picked it up and began to read. The very first chapter was on the lying tongue. Under the heading of the chapter title, were the words of Proverbs 12:22, "Lying lips *are* an abomination to the LORD, But those who deal truthfully *are* His delight." (NKJV) God wasted no time in using Scripture to say He hated my lying. Each day, I felt my conscious self speak to me. When I started to lie, I quickly said, "That's not true," or "That was a lie...the truth is..." And I corrected myself and spoke the truth.

Telling the truth blessed me in two ways. First, I no longer had to keep track of what I said for fear of getting caught in a lie, and second, I didn't have to feel guilty anymore. The value of the verse of the Gospel of John, "And you shall know the truth, and the truth shall make you free" (John 8:32 NKJV), became very clear to me.

God proceeded to mold me through people and circumstances. The first solid truth I began telling others was a real story about how I acquired the apartment my youngest son and I currently live in.

Back in October 2008, after the restraining order was released, I returned to my childhood home to temporarily reside with my parents until I could find a place for my children and me. I still faced criminal charges and my husband continued to blame me. He would not stop abusing prescription medication. Therefore, I couldn't return to our home to live with him. My parents allowed me to reside with them to save money and regain my strength. Yet, I needed to be independent. So, I offered a large deposit on a studio apartment to a landlord. I was greatly concerned about moving into the studio apartment. It was costly and very small. And I worried about modesty around my two sons. We would share one room to dress, eat, sleep and live in. The bathroom itself was tiny and semiprivate. However, I accepted the studio apartment because I was sure my past credit problems and low credit score would deny me a better option.

Just before moving into the studio, I met with the landlord and explained my reservations. She was very understanding. She handed me my uncashed deposit check without hesitation. I stayed with my parents and continued to look for another, more suitable, apartment.

In December 2008, the criminal case was dropped. I enthusiastically called a property management company and submitted an application for a two bedroom apartment. Within a week, the office staff offered the two bedroom apartment to me. It seemed impossible with my poor credit. Curiosity ran deep. So, I asked the staff member how I qualified for the larger apartment. She told me the day that she ran my credit, *all three* bureaus sites "were down for the day." My faith began to grow.

The rent was somewhat more than the studio, but the deposit was $300.00 lower and the apartment came with a walk-in closet and two over-sized bathrooms. I knew God had worked His miracle and that He was by my side. I immediately moved in and I was home.

Another story I love to tell is about my first Christmas in the apartment. When I moved, I grabbed most of our Christmas decorations. I had purchased them prior to marrying my husband. And with very little furniture, I needed something to make the cold apartment feel warm. Garland and little white lights decorated the empty spaces and the apartment felt like a home. I drove over to a local Christmas tree farm in search of the biggest tree I could to find to fill the empty living room. There, a gentleman was willing to discount the tree and even transport it to the apartment for me at no charge. I was moved by his generosity and kept telling others about what God had done for me. The surprising ending to this story is that that Christmas tree farm has not existed since December 2008. Had God placed that man there just for me?

Then, God used my love of watching movies to reach me about telling the truth. When I first moved into the apartment, I could only afford internet, not cable television. After completing homework assignments online, I would stream movies and television shows through the internet. Because it was Christmas time, I watched the movie "The Nativity Story." I wondered what Mary, the mother of God, must have endured in carrying her baby-the Son of God! I began to deeply appreciate Mary for her choice to tell the truth, and at such a young age, to her family and others about being pregnant with the Lord. She didn't concern herself with what others' thought. Joseph too, the earthly father of Christ, would have changed history if he had lied about the person Jesus would become. I am certain that telling the truth, God's Truth, was difficult for Mary and Joseph to do. But where would we be today had they lied?

I am grateful that God uses an average person like me to tell His truth and witness to others about His unending goodness. Even now, it saddens me at how many times I lied to avoid embarrassment and how many times my lies must have personally told God that His truth was not good enough. I now believe all of the tough events in my life could have been used to Glorify God. I wasted too much time worrying, feeling depressed and alone and making up stories to get people to like me instead of living my life according to His will, His story for me.

Over the past two years, instead of entertaining people with *my* stories, and then walking away feeling gratification for my ego, I tell God's story for me. I witness to how He is touching my life with His truth. In the process, God touches the lives of others.

It greatly amazes me that in just telling the truth, a total stranger will tear up, get the "goose bumps" or become more hopeful.

Sometimes when I start to talk about God with a total stranger, it even feels as if the stranger was waiting for me to come along. There is an instant feeling of comfort between us and often I hear the stranger say, "I don't believe this was an accident that we met today." The incredible part is that sharing my testimony to receptive strangers can only be explained by God's divine intervention. I am convinced that I must always speak in truth, both God's truth for me and His truth as told by His only Son, my Savior, Jesus Christ.

I Love to Tell the Story
Text: Katherine Hankey, 1866
Music: William G. Fisher, 1869

I love to tell the story
of unseen things above,
of Jesus and his glory,
of Jesus and his love.
I love to tell the story,
because I know 'tis true;
it satisfies my longings
as nothing else can do.

I love to tell the story,
'twill be my theme in glory,
to tell the old, old story
of Jesus and his love.
I love to tell the story;
more wonderful it seems
than all the golden fancies
of all our golden dreams.
I love to tell the story,
it did so much for me;
and that is just the reason
I tell it now to thee.

I love to tell the story;
'tis pleasant to repeat
what seems, each time I tell it,
more wonderfully sweet.
I love to tell the story,
for some have never heard

the message of salvation
from God's own holy Word.

I love to tell the story,
for those who know it best
seem hungering and thirsting
to hear it like the rest.
And when, in scenes of glory,
I sing the new, new song,
'twill be the old, old story
that I have loved so long.

CHAPTER SEVENTEEN

FROM SATAN'S HELPER TO GOD'S WARRIOR

Ephesians 6:10-13 Finally, my brethren, be strong in the Lord and in the power of His might. Put on the whole armor of God that you may be able to stand against the wiles of the devil. For we do not wrestle against flesh and blood, but against principalities, against powers, against the rulers of the darkness of this age, against spiritual hosts of wickedness in the heavenly places. Therefore take up the whole armor of God, that you may be able to withstand in the evil day, and having done all, to stand (NKJV).

The first time I became an eye witness to Satan's schemes was on the night I was arrested. Until that time, I viewed Satan as a distant character, not relevant to my life. Of course, I didn't know scripture then. All I knew was he was cast out of Heaven and God was more powerful than him. I thought many times, "How strong could he be?" I didn't comprehend, how I had to stand firm against his strategies and tricks. It wasn't until I experienced his presence personally that I was no longer able to deny his evil nature or reality and his influence on me to sin.

Just minutes after the deputy brought me from our home to the patrol car, I looked back at my husband standing approximately 20 feet away. The porch light was shining on his face and revealed his rigid and unyielding posture. The deputy then told me I was going to jail. I responded, "Sir, please talk to my husband. He wouldn't want this." As the deputy put the cuffs on my wrists, he said, "Your husband was the one who told us to arrest you. He showed us the scratch marks on his chest and arms and said you did it. He also told us that you threw objects at him and threatened him with violence."

I wanted to defend myself. I attempted to retell the real truth but the deputy smugly interrupted and said, "You are going to jail. You can go the hard way or the easy way!" I placed my hands behind my back and the deputy snapped the cuffs on. I then bowed my head and prayed the Lord's Prayer out loud.

Again, I sought out my husband. This time, we locked eyes. I was hoping in my heart that he would come to the police car and admit what he had done.

Instead, he just stared intently back at me and folded his arms across his chest in a hateful gesture.

I will never forget the look in my husband's eyes that night. His sinfully proud glare was shocking. He was clearly rejoicing in my suffering. I kept repeating to myself and the deputies, "That is not my husband." In a very real way, that night, the spiritual world became my visual reality. In that moment, I couldn't see any of my own failings, but my husband's actions revealed how his heart was penetrated with sin. Both our pride and selfishness almost destroyed our marriage.

After this night, I could no longer deny the power of sin and the existence of Satan. By writing this chapter, I do not give Satan free rein. I don't believe everything bad stems from Satan's schemes. I do believe though, Satan is prowling around when I felt tempted or distracted. I also know when I call upon God for help, He rescues me and Satan fades away.

A few months after my arrest, I started taking classes in the Seminarian program. Through class assignments, I read about biblical spiritual battles. I believe now my marriage was a battlefield against God.

During our courtship, my husband agreed to participate in premarital counseling with the Base Chaplain. At the time, I professed to be a Christian and felt my husband should verbally commit his life and our marriage to God. After a few months, my husband acknowledged I was a Christian and planned to live as a Christian too. I trusted that a commitment made through a few statements about God was all that was necessary and proper.

Within the first few months of our marriage we were challenged regarding our faith. We became pregnant soon after the wedding but had a miscarriage only six weeks later. I waited so long for a child and felt devastated by the loss.

My husband had lost his first son as a toddler. The sadness from our miscarriage seemed to surface the pain he felt from the loss of his first son. At first, my husband hid his feelings and showed me compassion. But when his own pain multiplied, he lost control. He became angry and we began to emotionally and spiritually tear apart. My husband turned to self-medicate; I sought prayer.

Although we both agreed to allow time to heal from our loss, God knew my heart best and we became pregnant again right away. While pregnant, I accepted a new job at the local base chapel. I related with fellow church members and found myself joyful and fired up for God. I was thrilled to be pregnant and I loved my new job!

I nervously watched my husband's drinking and gambling increase. Day by day, he became angrier with me. As I gained weight during the pregnancy, he cracked "fat jokes" around the house. He encouraged hatred from his children directed towards me. If he wasn't putting me down, he was giving me the silent treatment.

At the same time, I found comfort in church. I taught Vacation Bible School (VBS) and began to sing songs filled with scripture around our house.

This seemed to fuel my husband's anger. Now, nothing I did was good enough for him. Suddenly, my cooking was awful, the house was not clean enough and I talked too much. When I encouraged my husband to share his feelings, he became terribly irritable and angry.

After several months of this verbal abuse, I felt angry too. I became defensive, sarcastic and controlling. I suggested we try counseling. Unfortunately, I was too self-righteous in my opinions and disliked the few counselors we met with. We only attended a few sessions. Eventually, we just stopped talking, period. I participated in additional church activities while my husband made extra trips to the golf course and drank.

Six months pregnant, I thought, "No more!" I told my husband I was going to a shelter. I couldn't accept our stifling and unhappy marriage any longer. He asked me to stay and offered to attend church with me on Easter and Christmas. I was thrilled to have him by my side in church, even if he was going as a "favor" to me.

As the years passed, we became desensitized to the fighting. We chose our battles. However, our fights over Christianity and its role in our home, continued. Church on Easter and Christmas was it for my husband. No talk of Christ was permitted in our home. This banned movies about Christ, what I learned in church, spiritual songs being played on the radio: everything.

My husband was consistently angry and distant. Eventually, I grew weary by his rejection and started to feel isolated. I was exhausted from my attempt to lead my husband to Christ. I felt depressed. I knew I had no biblical reason to divorce my husband. As far as I knew, he had not committed adultery. In my mind, I had lost this battle. I had married an unbeliever, and he would remain an unbeliever, forever. I was stuck!

I was convinced that my marriage was doomed to fail. Yet, I didn't run to God for help. Instead, I desperately sought after my husband's approval. I focused all of my attention on my husband instead of worshipping God. I was determined to make my marriage work.

I started accompanying my husband to a casino to gamble. We watched movies I knew were wrong. I overate, attended church less and less and cursed often. I also told inappropriate jokes. It didn't take too long before I had become everything I warned my husband about. I was miserable!

One night alone in our bedroom, I watched television and played games on my laptop. A short documentary was on a channel. The featured doctors asked for donations for the country of Haiti. I recalled happy memories of a mission trip I took years prior. I wanted to be happy like this again and prayed for God to use me to help others in need. *Four days later*, my husband overdosed on prescription medication and physically hurt me.

On the day I was arrested, I looked inward and saw how pride, self-righteousness, judgment and arrogance had taken over my heart. It was instantly crystal clear to me that the end result of choosing

Satan's path, the world and another man over God, led to suffering and hopelessness.

When I felt Jesus' presence in jail later that night, I committed my future to God. I listed all of the many ways that I had let Satan rule over my heart. And, I told God I was sorry. Once and for all, I picked the correct team. I picked God. I made a public profession of my faith. My husband followed my lead.

At work, after several attempts, my husband finally accepted an invitation from his supervisor to attend his church. Our sons and I were included as well. I was still cautious around my husband, so I drove my own car and met him at his supervisor's church.

We sat together and listened while the Pastor spoke about forgiveness. At the end of his sermon, the Pastor asked his wife up to the podium. She addressed the congregation and compelled anyone who was carrying the weight of a heavy burden to lay it down before God. She asked God to forgive those sins. Her words quietly yet firmly reached through to my husband's heart. He started to stumble and his supervisor and I moved to catch him as he fell. We laid our caring hands on my husband's broad shoulders as he knelt and sobbed. I felt moved by the sweet sound of his tears.

After church, I followed my husband's truck to our home. When I arrived, I noticed my husband still sitting in his truck. I walked up to the truck and opened the driver's door. My husband had both hands gripping the steering wheel and he was weeping as he listened to a song, "Live Like You Were Dying," by Tim McGraw. That day, my husband accepted Christ into his heart. It was a miraculous and joyous moment for me. I was amazed!

My husband started attending church each Wednesday night. Through Christ, we began to slowly lay a foundation for our marriage. As we both healed from past pain, our marriage healed too. Certainly, I thought, a defeated Satan had departed from my life.

Unfortunately though, Satan did not go away. However, God protected me and provided a way of escape. He did not allow temptation beyond what I was able to handle.

On one attempt, Satan manipulated my youngest son to hurt me. At the time, my husband and I had been talking about finding a new home together. However, his employer called and told him that he was immediately needed to supervise a crew of men assigned to clean up a recent gulf coast oil spill. The job was located miles across the United States. Without much option, my husband moved to Florida with an unexpected return date. He flew home once a month for a few days to be with us.

During this time, my youngest son begged me daily to stay home from preschool. He said some boys in his class were mean. On his last day of pre-school, I watched my son approach three boys and ask if he could play with them. They told him, "No." So, he asked if he could watch them play. The boys then told my son he couldn't even watch them play. This rejection broke my heart. Since summer was approaching, I kept him home and home schooled my son.

When the new school year began, I considered my alternatives. We were uncertain whether my husband would return to our home state. I just couldn't justify driving twenty minutes back and forth and paying the school's high tuition since my son clearly disliked the school. We temporarily placed our son in public school while we waited for a permanent work assignment.

My son instantly loved his new kindergarten class and teachers. He made several new friends and couldn't wait to go school each day. For the first time, he was returning home from school happy. He was interested in what he was learning and talked about friends he had played with during the day. Unfortunately, my son also brought home, new sayings and a very challenging attitude.

During the second month of school, my son began to act out. It started one day, just after he woke up. My five-year-old was talking back to me! I was quite surprised since this behavior was contrary to his normal respectful attitude. Rather than hug me good morning as usual, with his baby blanket in arm, he walked straight past me and sat on the couch. His ugly attitude continued as I walked him to his kindergarten class. And, as soon as he returned home, he appeared rejuvenated with an even worse tongue. He repeatedly said, "You can't make me," to simple requests like, "Please put your lunchbox on the counter." In one day, I had sent my son to more disciplinary timeouts than in an entire year. I retreated to think, "Where is my son, and who is this little person?"

The next day, he started throwing his toys and had a tantrum when I instructed him to get ready for school and eat his breakfast. His anger was escalating. By now, so was my frustration. Normally he was obedient. I couldn't believe we were having a power struggle.

On the third day, around bedtime, my son asked if he could sleep with his shirt off. I told him he had to wear his shirt to bed because the apartment was cold at night and I didn't want him to get sick. Unexpectedly, he said, "I want a new mommy!" His words shattered my heart. I was stunned and walked out of his room without finishing our normal bedtime prayer and routine. I cried, feeling lost.

By the fourth day, I struggled to keep my adult head together. My son continued talking back and saying hurtful things, such as, "I want to go live with my daddy." I told him I didn't like the way he was treating me. He was acting downright mean. I asked about his school day and how the other kids behaved in class. "Are you copying someone in class who acts mean? Are you being picked on? Did someone hurt you?" He just shook his head, "No" to each question. *He* even seemed confused by his behavior.

I began to sing, "Put on the full armor of God, so that you can take your stand, against the devil's schemes... be strong in the Lord." My son sang the first part with me as he loves and knows the song well. During the song, I took a washable marker from the kitchen table to draw muscles on his arms and a shield on his chest with the word "GOD" across the shield. In my best Arnold Schwarzenegger voice, I mimicked, "Oh you have big muscles for God." He laughed his normal laugh.

But then my son looked down at his chest, took the darkest colored marker from the table, and drew a big "X" across the word God. I sent him to bed, feeling very discouraged.

After he fell asleep that night, I went into his room to pick up his clothes. The pictures of our family on his dresser were lying face down. I left his room feeling emotionally and physically exhausted. What was going on?

My first thought was to consider the impact of his father's absence. But, then, we hadn't lived with my husband in over a year and a half. Was he was feeling lost in public school? Finally, I excused his behavior as a result of being tired and adjusting to a new schedule. I reinstated naptime. However, when he woke up from naps just as cranky and disrespectful, I ran out of excuses.

Feeling discouraged, I confided in a friend for help. This particular friend holds a special place in my heart. She was the one I called upon my release from jail. Even though it was late at night and she had never driven without her husband at such a late hour, she insisted on being there to comfort me. I will never forget the gift of her sitting by my side and holding my hand in the lobby of the jail. She remained by my side as I waited for my parents to arrive. That night, we became more than work associates. Later, she would teach me about Scripture and encourage my walk with Christ. I came to rely on her for spiritual guidance as well as friendship in my life.

So naturally, I called this friend to discuss my youngest son. She listened quietly as she had always done. Then she spoke about spiritual battles. She asked if I thought my son was battling against me because I was writing this book to worship the Lord. In her usual sweet demeanor, she offered to pray for my son. She called on the Lord and asked Him to visit my son in his dreams. I cried as she spoke. Her prayer was comforting and instantly eased my anxiety. She also prayed for God's protection for me.

When she finished praying, my friend suggested that I pray for my son while he slept. After we ended the call, I took my bible to my son's room. He was fast asleep. I made a cross on his forehead and chest and then prayed a very simple prayer, "God, please help me to help my son."

The next day, my son woke up and he was silent. Although he was not acting his usual jovial self, he was no longer acting disrespectful either. As he dressed, I erased all of the names on my prayer board and put my son's name across the board in large letters. I told him what I did. He lit up! He hugged me very tightly around the neck as he questioned, "What about the others?" I replied, "*You* need my prayers right now."

My son put his jacket on for school. He then looked at the prayer board. He erased his name and wrote it again in even larger letters. Then he threw the hood of the jacket off his head, and said, "I am so mad right now." I thought, here we go again!

I calmly asked, "What's wrong?" He said, "I am so mad at the devil for using me to say mean things to my mommy." My five-year-old son: so insightful. My eyes welled with tears. I put my hands down, palm side up. He quickly slapped me "five." In that moment, we were back to normal.

We drove to school, and there he asked the other children if they believed in God. One child said he believed in dinosaurs. My son told him about God as they rolled their hula hoops around the blacktop. In the car, I silently thanked God for protecting my family from the devil's schemes.

In the months to come, I continually face situations requiring God's intervention. Each time, I prayed and relied on God. God responded and provided protection. As a result, I began to see attacks as an opportunity to declare God's mighty power.

One day, while writing another chapter of this book and as the words of praise towards God poured out on paper, I heard the phone ring. I answered the phone thinking perhaps my husband was calling long distance. I heard a female voice and her words were broken. It sounded as if a cell phone had a bad connection. I could hear someone moaning and instantly knew that it was an obscene call.

In the past, I would have been angry and upset. I would say, "I am a Social Worker, I know all the judges and your call is being traced." Of course, the only truth was my position as a Social Worker. I didn't know the judges and could not trace a call. But it was an effective method and usually stopped crank callers from calling back. However, this time, when she had paused, I said, "It sounds like you need prayer right now. Do you want me to pray with you?" The caller hung up.

I returned to the desk to resume writing when the phone rang a second time. I checked caller ID and it read "private caller." Incredibly, I remained calm. I answered the phone and the same voice asked, "So are you interested?" The call was much clearer now; I even heard background noises. Out loud, I prayed, "Please Lord Jesus, help this girl who feels that she needs to do this right now. Please Lord Jesus! I ask this in your precious name, Amen." It sounded like she was crying before she hung up for the second time. I hadn't fought evil with evil. I was compassionate and I sought God to help me fight against the ugliness.

I looked at the picture of Jesus on my wall and said, "Lord, please work on her heart today. Convict her Jesus, so much, that she cannot make another call, even if she doesn't know why. Let her tell this story when she receives Your grace. Thank you for allowing me to glorify you. Thank you for working through me and directing her to call *me* today. What a blessing! Thank you Lord." Amen.

Satan continued his schemes, but the attacks seemed like mere harassment. For instance, my cross necklace fell off my neck the day I was baptized. There was nothing wrong with the clasp and I had worn the necklace without fail for several years. But on the day of my baptism, the cross necklace fell straight to the ground. I giggled at his minor attempt to take my focus from God and used the situation to further praise God. The day was perfect. I even felt complete relief from pain I experienced the day before.

Then on another day, while talking about our Holy God with a neighbor, I was attacked by bees. A bee even tried to fly up my dress. Again, I laughed at this ineffective attempt to interrupt my praise and worship of God. I continued to praise God to the new believer in front of me. I said "I'm not going to stop praising God because of a little bee sting." My neighbor watched as the bees bounced off me like flies. I wasn't stung, not even once.

Even though these attacks by Satan are minor, I believe they were meant to prepare me. I am uncertain what the future holds, but I know I am called to evangelize, no matter the cost. Perhaps the lessons over the years were devised by God's plan to strengthen me for what is to come.

I am confident that I made the right choice in surrendering my life to God and have lost the desire to sin. Trust is overcoming my anxiety and I finally feel at peace. I am surrendering every area of my life: my secrets, my sins and my rebellion to God's will. In Christ Alone I choose to move confidently forward into the next phase of my journey. He is my strength, my hope and my light!

Post Script

As I finished writing this chapter, claiming my love and commitment to Christ, another amazing thing happened. I looked outside my kitchen door and noticed two white and gray doves crossing the street towards me. They were walking slowly. My immediate concern was that they would get hit by a car so I tried to coax them across the street. They continued to walk leisurely towards my door. The moment made an impression on me so I decided to grab my camera. Unfortunately, the doves flew away before I could take a picture. I was curious as to the meaning of two doves. I went to the computer and searched online for the significance of two doves. The explanation I found for the meaning of two doves together was simple. Two doves represented *"everlasting love."*

Here I was writing a chapter on my devotion towards God and in another meaningful way, God confirmed He loves me too. I know God will remain with me always. His love endures forever!

I Surrender All

Text: J.W. VenDeVenter, 1896
Music: W.S. Weeden

All to Jesus I surrender;
all to him I freely give;
I will ever love and trust him,
in his presence daily live.

I surrender all, I surrender all,
all to thee, my blessed Savior,
I surrender all.

CHAPTER EIGHTEEN

THE HOLY SPIRIT LIVES WITHIN ME

Acts 5:32 And we are His witnesses to these things, and *so* also *is* the Holy Spirit whom God has given to those who obey Him (NKJV).

I was required to write a research paper about the deity and personality of the Holy Spirit. Many hours of research and contemplation led me to one conclusion. The Holy Spirit was active within my own life. God was bestowing Him upon me to convince others of His presence.

The second year after the arrest rolled around. By now, it was very natural to bring up God in conversations throughout the day. I no longer worried about rejection or those embarrassing feelings and watched in wonder as many people were comforted to hear about God and His presence. On many occasions, it felt as if someone was waiting for me to tell them God is alive and cares for them. Meanwhile, God was blessing me regularly with the gift of wise counsel from spiritual friends and the words sung to me in church. Through reassurance and blessings, God continued to compel me to tell others about Him.

Each day, I humbly asked the Holy Spirit to help me in some meaningful way to touch the lives of others. On several occasions, He responded and communicated His will to my heart.

On one occasion, while enjoying warm drinks with my five-year-old son at a local coffee house, a group of six men entered the store dressed in suits and ties. This was an unlikely situation for our small town. I figured the men were either from a church congregation or employed with the County. Since one of the men appeared too young to be a County employee, I concluded they were from a church.

I hadn't taken much time to dress nicely or do my hair or make up that day. It was a weekday, midmorning, and I was alone in the coffee house with my son. Both of us were dressed casual. Perhaps the men in this group thought I was an unemployed, unwed, single-mother. A few of them looked over at us repeatedly as they stood in line to order their drinks.

In my hand, I held a book assigned for an evangelism class through the seminary program. The book encouraged readers to start conversations with others about Jesus and allow the Holy Spirit to do the rest.

I was trying to finish reading the book by the day's end.

One of the men standing in the group at the counter and I had made eye contact. As he walked by our table he looked eager to speak with me. He began the conversation by asking where I was from. I told him I lived locally. I then asked if his group was part of a congregation. He said they attended the Kingdom Hall a few blocks away from the coffee house. When he asked if my son and I attended a church, I told him that our family attended the Calvary Chapel down the same street. The man stared at me with a look of disappointment as he walked on by. The rest of his group followed him and walked past our table. They sat huddled around a small table in the corner a few feet away.

My son and I remained at our table another ten minutes before I felt the Holy Spirit in my heart say, "Please pray with this group of men." So, I put my book down and told my son what I intended to do and he became excited. We walked over to their table and I said, "Excuse me, I don't mean to bother you, but would you mind if my son and I prayed with you?" The man, who I had spoken with minutes prior, swallowed his bite of food and quickly responded, "That won't be necessary." I was taken aback. For almost two years, not one person had said "No" to me when I asked to pray with them, so I thought I must have heard him wrong. Out of disbelief, I said, "I'm sorry?" He simply repeated, "That won't be necessary."

I could tell that he stood alone in this decision because another man who was sitting across the table from the man speaking winked at me and smiled at my 5-year-old son. However, being sensitive to the Holy Spirit, it was clear that this was all I was supposed to do. I said "Okay, God bless you," and turned to leave. My young son, innocently and very loudly, asked, "Aren't we going to pray with them?" I told him, "Not here, but yes, we will definitely pray for them in the car."

I don't know why this man rejected prayer. Nor do I comprehend the prompting of the Holy Spirit through me in approaching this group of men. I felt self-conscious as I opened the door to exit the coffee house. Within seconds though, while explaining to my son why a group of sharply dressed men refused to pray with us, I felt a calmness and sense of joy. I told my son, "We may never know why we are prompted to do things for God and it is okay. All we have to do is obey and respond to His call."

Soon after, God provided another opportunity for me to share His presence. One day, while walking to his truck, my husband found a child's wallet. He brought the wallet to me. We looked inside to find an address or phone number for the owner. Yet all we found was a school identification card and $9.00. I searched for child's the last name in the local phone book. One number was listed with the same last name. I called the number but the man who answered did not know the child.

I held onto the wallet for a few days while I deliberated how to return it to its owner. Then, I had an overwhelming feeling that I should place additional money in the wallet. I went to the bank, withdrew $20.00 and placed the money inside. I attached a note to the $20.00. On a small yellow post-it, I wrote, "God loves you." Then I went to the child's school and returned the wallet. Before leaving the receptionist's office, I told her what I had done. She appeared stunned. She said, "I am not used to that type of honesty. I will make sure the boy receives his wallet. Thank you."

At a later time, I woke to a woman crying out for help from across the street. It was pouring rain when I went to my back door patio to investigate. I could barely see all that was happening. Through the rain, it appeared as though other neighbors were attempting to help a woman remove two aggressive males from her home.

I felt my normal instinct command me to impulsively get involved. However, in the past, this response only led to further confusion and chaos. Instead, I started to pray. "Lord, rid me of myself and have me respond to Your will." I immediately felt my feet become heavy, as though I was standing in drying cement. I thought, "Obviously, I am to remain still." I continued to pray. "Lord, please let the boys leave now." Immediately after I ended my prayer, I watched as the aggressive males ran from the woman's home. They jumped into their pick up truck and drove away quickly. Then, the local police arrived.

The next day, I began my day as usual, quietly reading God's word. The memory of the night of October 20, 2008, interrupted my thoughts. My heart filled with empathy for the frantic woman from the night prior. Then God placed within my heart, a very strong desire to write the woman a letter. I placed my bible in front of me while I sat at my computer and began to write.

"Blessings,

Last night I heard you cry out for help. I woke up to your screams and immediately began to pray. I live across the street and was able to see your balcony from my back porch. It appeared that there were several people helping you force the boys to leave.

Rather than leave my six-year-old unattended, I stood on my back porch and began to pray. I prayed this prayer. "Heavenly Father, please help my neighbor. Make the teenagers leave. Please Father, let her know that you are there with her and help comfort her. Please protect this woman and keep her safe. I ask this in your precious Son's name, Amen."

I stayed on my porch wondering if I should get involved. There was a man who came out to chase the boys away. I continued to pray. "Please, Heavenly Father, let the boys leave now, without incident. Amen." Praise God, they left.

God has placed a need on my heart to write to you today. It was not long ago that I moved into my apartment because of violence. If you need me to continue to pray that you feel safe and protected or for any other reason, please do not hesitate to call. My number is …

In the love of Christ, your neighbor,

I went across the street to deliver the letter. I knocked on several doors before finding the right apartment. As the single-mother opened the door, her small child nudged her little head through her mother's legs, and said, "You wanna come inside?" I bent over to tell the child, "No thank you," then I smiled and handed the woman the letter. I explained how I had prayed for her safety. Through her tears, the woman whispered words of gratitude.

On another occasion, I felt the Spirit inspire me to bring the Word of God to one particular homeless man. As a new child of Christ, I wrestled with how to humbly spread the gospel to others. I felt inadequate to speak scripture to anyone. Yet, I couldn't deny the presence of the Holy Spirit and felt I couldn't keep quiet. So one day, I recorded a taped message for the elderly man. I used an old, hand held tape recorder and asked my five-year-old son to create a message. My son spoke into the recorder and told the man that we loved him and that he can come to our home any-time. He even added the name of the city and state we live in. Then I recorded my message. I said that we loved him and that God loves him too and has not forgotten him. I put the tape recorder in my car and started to look for the homeless man.

It took weeks of driving around town before we found him and gave him the taped gift. I also gave him a used bible. I played the message and parroted what my son said. The elderly man, with his long white beard, began to cry. He confided through his tears, that he had been recently questioning his exis-tence and feeling very depressed. I began to cry also.

As the tears rolled down our cheeks, I watched as he passed his weathered fingers over the words "Holy Bible" on the front cover. He lost his composure and I could tell that he was embarrassed by the out-pouring of tears. He asked me to stay with him until he was able to regain his composure. I stayed.

Not much time had passed before I felt the warmth of the Holy Spirit again. By this time, I had learned to say "okay" to those goose bumps and nudges. In that instant, I felt His presence prompt me to offer peace to a man in my town. One day while driving my youngest son to the local coffee house for a treat of hot chocolate, a man cut me off in my car. He appeared in a great hurry. Rather than cause trouble as I would have before, all I wanted to do now was to mirror God's peace. But the man raced past the stop and was nowhere to be found.

So, I drove towards the local coffee house. As God would have it, when I glanced up at the car before me in the drive-thru, it was the same man! I told my youngest son what I was going to do, got out of my car, then went to this stranger's window and explained, "Sir, I am Donna. You just cut me off back there. It seems like you are having a rough morning already. Can I buy your cup of coffee today?" His eyes became really big before he politely refused and dropped his head. When he drove up to the window to pay for his order, he was extremely polite and soft spoken to the employee. I thanked God as I observed the man drive away slowly.

Still, my favorite story involves a crossing guard at my son's elementary school. One day while driving my son to kindergarten, I felt a tug on my heart to purchase a cup of coffee for one particular crossing guard. We had almost pulled up to the school when the feeling became undeniable. I turned my car around and headed for the local coffee house. I purchased a cup of regular drip coffee and returned to the school. Then I walked to the crosswalk where the woman was standing. As I offered her the cup of coffee, she cried out, "Oh my gosh!" I all but spilled the coffee on both of us. She said in a surprised tone, "You are not going to believe this, but I just texted my friend and told her I needed a cup of coffee. I can't believe you just handed me a cup. I just texted her a second ago!" I told the woman I believe in God and felt a desire to buy her coffee today. She affirmed that she is a believer in our Lord Jesus Christ. With a single cup of coffee, God had confirmed our belief!

Since October 2008, I have learned to obey the Holy Spirit and follow His prompting when sharing Christ with others. When He compels me to act, I obey without questioning Him and without understanding His reasons. Sometimes God reveals to me later the "why." Other times, I am left to trust that the Holy Spirit is leading me to God's plan for me.

I am delighted at how God coordinates perfect opportunities for me to share with others about Him. I feel eternally grateful that God allows the Holy Spirit to live within me. Thank you God!

Have Thine Own Way, Lord
Text: Adelaide A. Pollard, 1862-1934
Music: George C. Stebbins, 1846-1945

Have thine own way, Lord! Have thine own way!
Thou art the potter, I am the clay.
Mold me and make me after thy will,
while I am waiting, yielded and still.

Have thine own way, Lord! Have thine own way!
Search me and try me, Savior today!
Wash me just now, Lord, wash me just now,
as in thy presence humbly I bow. Have thine own
way, Lord!

Have thine own way!
Wounded and weary, help me I pray!
Power, all power, surely is thine!
Touch me and heal me, Savior divine! Have thine
own way, Lord!

Have thine own way!
Hold o'er my being absolute sway.
Fill with thy Spirit till all shall see
Christ only, always, living in me!

CHAPTER NINETEEN

I AM BLESSED

Matthew 5:3-10 Blessed are the poor in spirit, For theirs is the kingdom of heaven. Blessed are those who mourn, For they shall be comforted. Blessed are the meek, For they shall inherit the earth. Blessed are those who hunger and thirst for righteousness, For they shall be filled. Blessed are the merciful, For they shall obtain mercy. Blessed are the pure in heart, For they shall see God. Blessed are the peacemakers, For they shall be called sons of God. Blessed are those who are persecuted for righteousness' sake, For theirs is the kingdom of heaven (NKJV).

While attending mass as a child and later participating in the church choir, I often sang the song, "*Blessed are they*. " The words to the song are, "Blessed are they, the poor in spirit, theirs is the kingdom of God. Blessed are they, full of sorrow, they shall be consoled. Rejoice and be glad! Blessed are you, holy are you, Rejoice and be glad! Yours is the kingdom of God!"

As a little child, I was unaware I was singing scripture straight from the Gospel of Matthew. However, since surrendering my life to Christ, I can testify to the truth of these words. I have been blessed! Just as Jesus promised in Scripture, when I am filled with sorrow, God consoles me. When I feel lowly and humbled, He exalts me. And when I feel empty, He fills me with the Holy Spirit. My life is a testimony to God's blessings. His presence is with me, and for the first time, I feel content.

O Holy Night
Text: Placide Clappeau, 1847
Music: Adolphe C. Adam (1803-1856)

O holy night, the stars are brightly shining;
It is the night of the dear Savior's birth!
Long lay the world in sin and error pining,
Till He appeared and the soul felt its worth.
A thrill of hope, the weary soul rejoices,
For yonder breaks a new and glorious morn.

Fall on your knees, O hear the angel voices!
O night divine, O night when Christ was born!
O night, O holy night, O night divine!

At Christmas, I sat in church listening to the choir sing, "Oh Holy Night." As I heard the words, "...long lay the world, in sin and err pinning, 'till He appeared, and the soul felt its worth," streams of tears started running down my cheeks. I realized my own soul finally felt its worth. These days, I am filled with hope and my soul rejoices.

Over the past two years, I have experienced God's mercy, the joy of favor, devotion, freedom and good health. This chapter could be considerably long if I attempted to include all of the blessings I have received over the past two years. I want to share a few of my favorites.

It was December 2008, a couple of months past the crisis with my husband. My husband still hadn't admitted to lying to his family about what happened in October. Therefore, I wasn't expecting to see or hear from any of his family members for a long time. For Christmas, however, my brother-in-law and his wife gave me a wonderful gift.

My husband and his brother work for the same company. At their annual Christmas party one night, I opened their gift. Nestled in the middle of white tissue paper was a statue made by a company named Willow Tree. The statue, "Angel's Embrace," was a carved angel holding a child. It stood only a few inches tall. The small statue brought me incredible comfort. In my mind, my own three- year-old son was surrounded by such loving hands during the week I was legally restrained from him in October. Each subsequent time I glanced at the statue, I was reminded that God held my son in His arms during the most trying times of my life.

On another occasion, God fixed my reading glasses. I did not have vision insurance when I began to write this book. I wore broken, miserable reading glasses. I found an optometrist. I went into the local doctor's office *just to price* the rubber pieces. I was still only working part-time and my savings account was running low. The optometrist's assistant greeted me at the door and asked to see my glasses. She started fixing my glasses. I felt butterflies in my stomach not knowing the cost. Then she adjusted the glasses to make them more comfortable for me. When she finished, she handed back my glasses and said, "Okay, here you go," and, "there's no charge." My eyes welled up with tears as I told her briefly how God had blessed me with her generosity.

Then it was almost Thanksgiving Day, and for the first time, after eight years, my stepson was not coming home for the holiday. I felt sad and the sting of rejection. I decided to go grocery shopping for a three person meal. As I pulled into the parking lot, I noticed a homeless man I didn't know. I pulled over to the curb and got out of my car. I handed the young man a bible and $5.00. After speaking with him for a few minutes I began to testify to him about God's love. I was pleasantly surprised when he said he was a Christian too. I gave the young man my name and shook his hand. As we grasped hands, he looked at me with wonder in his eyes. He then asked, "You're Donna?" After I nodded "Yes," he said, "I have heard about you." He proceeded to tell me how

I was loved by one particular homeless man in our town. My heart melted. I cried all the way home that day, thanking God that I was making a difference in someone's life. I thanked God for the blessing of that conversation. God knew the perfect way to lift my spirit. I thanked God for the freedom to share His love and compassion with others.

Soon after, God blessed me on the drive to work. For many days, I had prayed for two particular friends to feel the presence of God. They were experiencing a rough time. One day, I specifically prayed, "Please God, won't you restore their confidence? Please let them know you are near." Then, I hurried off to work. For miles along the highway, I sung the same three spiritual songs at the top of my lungs. It was time to exit.

When I pulled up to the first stoplight and the bustle of my engine quieted, I noticed immediately that the volume of my radio was blasting. I glanced into the next car as I started to turn the music down. I noticed the woman in the truck beside my car was singing in harmony with the song that played from my radio. I watched in amazement as she mouthed the words, "I'm desperate for you, and I...I'm lost without you." My eyes welled with tears. God had made Himself known to me! I removed my sunglasses to make direct eye contact with the woman. With tears streaming down my face, I whispered, "Thank you." My offer of gratitude seemed to strike a chord with the woman, who also began to cry.

Another blessing rose from a tragedy. In 2009, a young man was riding his new motorcycle past our home. He hit a curve in the road at a dangerous speed and lost control of the bike. The young man lost his life. A small cross was placed on the side of the road where the accident occurred. For months, my young son and I pulled over and prayed next to the cross. In prayer, we asked God to comfort the family members of the twenty one-year-old.

Then one day, I noticed a man clearing the weeds from around the small wooden cross. He was moving unhurriedly and held his head low. I approached the man and introduced myself. He said he was the young man's father. I cried as he spoke about his love for his son. Then I said, "We have been praying for you." The man looked at me surprised and said, "I have felt your prayers, please don't stop." I welcomed the man to our home for dinner, but he kindly refused and continued to pull weeds. His name remains on my prayer board today.

Another blessing was watching my young son boldly speak the words of Luke 2:15 in front of a packed church. It was my son's first Christmas play. He had eagerly waited to play the role of a shepherd in the annual church production of *The Nativity Story*. He couldn't wait to tell others about God. He quickly learned his line and proudly announced it to anyone who would listen. He said, "Let us now go to Bethlehem and see this thing that has happened which the Lord has made known to us!" The night of the play, another little shepherd boy began to cry. The other child explained to my son how much *he* wanted the speaking role. With tears in his eyes, my six-year-old son, said, "If you want to say the line, you can. It's okay." What a sacrifice!

When the children took their places in front of the church, I was sure the other child would enjoy the speaking part. However, the microphone was handed to my child. He spoke clearly and slowly. When he finished his line, the whole congregation stood, clapped, whistled and screamed. What a blessing!

Perhaps my favorite gift from God came right before Christmas this year when I witnessed my young son's faith grow.

It was late Sunday afternoon when my husband drove back to his jobsite located three hours away. After my husband's temporary placement in Florida, his employer moved him back to California. Unfortunately, his new job site was still too far from home to commute each day. As a result, he only commuted home and stayed for the weekend.

After a few months of saying goodbye to his father every Sunday, the distance became too much. My young son had held in his feelings as long as he could. One Sunday, as he said "Goodbye" to his father, he began to cry. Because it was raining, my husband had decided to begin his long commute a little earlier than normal.

My son had been invited to a birthday party which was scheduled soon after we said "Goodbye." So, in my car, my son and I followed my husband's truck towards the freeway.

As we followed my husband's truck, my son continued to cry for his father. It broke my heart. I tried to make him laugh but my humor only distracted him for a minute or two before he resumed crying. I prayed out loud, "Dear Lord, your child needs you right now. Can you please let him know You are with him and will never leave him? Can You please let him feel Your arms around him? In Your precious name, Amen."

Through his tears, my six-year-old son said, "It's not working, I can't feel Him." I told him sometimes God's presence feels like goose bumps or a sweet feeling, or the warm touch of others. I told him to wait on the Lord.

We had two more freeway exits before arriving at the mall. I was curious when my husband exited the freeway right in front of us. He drove to the mall and parked near our car. He walked over to my son and said, "I don't care when I get to the hotel. You are more important than my job." He then reached out his hand and pulled my son to his side to hug him. My son looked at me and smiled. I knew what my son was thinking, "How did he know?"

When we entered the party, my shy son felt intimidated by the new environment. The father of the child who was celebrating her birthday walked over to greet us. I knew that the child's father suffered from intense back pain. Yet, he immediately got down on one knee, spread his hands wide and offered my son a hug. My husband was standing there to see the hug. By now, I couldn't help but tell the girl's father and my husband about the prayer I had just prayed in the car a few minutes earlier.

Eventually, it was time to leave the party. I asked my son if he needed to use the restroom before we drove back home. He said, "Yes." The nearest boy's bathroom was located in a large department store next to the party. As I walked my son to the restroom, we saw a man dressed as Santa Claus. I told my son I was going to say "Hi" to Santa. My son asked, "Why, isn't he just a man?" I knew that my son no longer believed in Santa Claus. Still, I felt compelled to go over to him and greet him. I shook Santa's hand and said, "Hi Santa." My son followed me and reached out *his* hand to shake Santa's hand. Santa, instead, knelt on the floor, on both knees and stretched his arms out wide. My son and I knew that God heard our simple prayer on the way to the party that day and that He was with us. In less than an hour and a half, God had wrapped His arms around my son three times.

Without a doubt, the greatest blessing I have received in my life is the gift of God's love and forgiveness! He has saved me from my sins, saved my marriage and saved others through His changes in me. He has taught me to trust and rest in Him. My feelings towards the work God has begun in me are sincerely expressed in the words of Isaiah 12: 1-2 (NKJV).

And in that day you will say:
"O LORD, I will praise You;
Though You were angry with me,
Your anger is turned away, and You comfort me.
Behold, God *is* my salvation,
I will trust and not be afraid;

169

'For YAH, the LORD, *is* my strength and song;
He also has become my salvation.'"

Each day, God continues to mold and shape my heart. I feel, He is not done with me yet. Rather, He has only just begun.

Just as two years ago, today, I find myself captivated by yet another television special about the country of Haiti. As I sit in my living room chair watching the special, I smile and begin to pray. I remember the last time I watched a special on Haiti and how I had prayed then for God to use me. This time with wisdom I prayed, "No matter what you want me to do, Lord I will do it! Please use me to bring others to You, so that I too may continue to change!" I wonder what God has planned for me next.

Blessed Assurance
Text: Fanny J. Crosby, 1820-1915
Music: Phoebe P. Knapp, 1839-1908

Blessed assurance, Jesus is mine!
what a foretaste of glory divine!
Heir of salvation, purchase of God,
born of his Spirit, washed in his blood.
This is my story, this is my song,
praising my Savior all the day long;
this is my story, this is my song,
praising my Savior all the day long.
Perfect submission, perfect delight,
visions of rapture now burst on my sight;
angels descending bring from above
echoes of mercy, whispers of love.

Perfect submission, all is at rest;
I in my Savior am happy and blest,
watching and waiting, looking above,
filled with his goodness, lost in his love.

ACKNOWLEDGEMENT

I want to honor a few people who supported me through my transformation. God used certain people to lead me spiritually, hold me up when I was weary, and provide a place of refuge for me to build strength and character.

I am sincerely grateful to my Pastor and his wife for their countless hours of prayers, compassion and Christian leadership. I would also like to thank my friends Victoria and Steve for their support and loving-kindness, my sister for her mercy and humor and my husband, children and best friend for forgiving my past ugliness.

I especially thank my mother and stepfather ("Dad"), whom without question demonstrated how a marriage can overcome obstacles and how to love and support even grown children. Finally, I thank my editor for her hard work, edification and encouragement while writing this book.

May the Lord bless you all for the love and support you provided to me through the years. To our Heavenly Father, I prayed this prayer for you.

Abba Father,

Please watch over my loved ones. Thank you for placing them in my life to teach me and nurture my heart. I deeply appreciate their love. Please reveal Your love for them each and everyday. Thank you Lord. I love You!

In your precious Son's name. Amen.

CPSIA information can be obtained
at www.ICGtesting.com
Printed in the USA
FSHW011951070119
54888FS

9 781613 791936